MILITARY INSTITUTIONS
AND COERCION
IN THE DEVELOPING NATIONS

T0294634

MILITARY INSTITUTIONS AND COERCION IN THE DEVELOPING NATIONS

MORRIS JANOWITZ

Expanded Edition of
*The Military in the Political Development
of New Nations*

THE UNIVERSITY OF CHICAGO PRESS

CHICAGO AND LONDON

Military Institutions and Coercion in the Developing Nations is an expanded edition of *The Military in the Political Development of New Nations*, originally published in 1964.

The University of Chicago Press, Chicago 60637
The University of Chicago Press, Ltd., London

Published 1964. Expanded edition 1977
Midway Reprint edition 1988
Printed in the United States of America

International Standard Book Number 0-226-39319-4
Library of Congress Catalog Card Number: 76-50462

CONTENTS

PREFACE, 1977

The original version of this work, titled *The Military in the Political Development of New Nations*, was published in 1964 as an outgrowth of my association with the Committee for Comparative Study of New Nations at the University of Chicago. A decade later it seemed appropriate to reexamine the original hypotheses which I offered in that essay.

The occasion for such a reexamination was the seminar in honor of Lloyd Fallers held in October 1975 on the campus of the University of Chicago. The continuing volume of writing on the military reinforced my concern with these issues. In particular, there were some excellent case studies which gave a sense of reality and depth to the conflicts and problems encountered by military regimes.

However, I did not give the topic the sustained attention which it required and warranted. My interests shifted to the United States society and to the United States military in the context of the political tensions of the welfare state and the shift to an all-volunteer military system. But it was clear, given my objectives—to assess the state of scholarship on the effect of the military on societal change in the developing nations—that it would not be meaningful to focus on my original hypotheses. Instead, or rather in addition, I had to proceed in broader terms. My original focus was on civil-military relations, and in particular on the central armed forces of the developing nations. After a decade I saw that I had to address the more encompassing issues of the changing patterns of coercion in these nation-states. This particularly required me to include the expansion of paramilitary forces, which have come to play an increasingly important role in the drift toward increased authoritarian rule.

Since the appearance of my original essay, there has been, in my judgment, a limited but discernible increase in the stability of the political regimes of these nation-states; one may at least speak of the consolidation of particular regimes. I was gradually drawn to the idea that the increase in size and effectiveness of paramilitary forces contributed over the short run to this trend. In my essay for the Fallers seminar I sought to marshal the evidence in support of this general hypothesis. At the same time, I was also impressed by the converging idea that the process of regime consolidation resulted in part from the more limited and more realistic goals national leaders came to adopt.

As a result, in reviewing the literature that has been produced on the political behavior of the military, I have come to believe that my original formulations have been accurately utilized by regionally and nationally oriented scholars. Their efforts to test these hypotheses have been rewarding and in fact exciting, since they have greatly enriched my formulations. By contrast, the efforts of "theoreticians" in comparative politics to make use of these propositions—to accept them, modify them, or reject them —have been much less rewarding. All too often their conceptual debates have produced intellectual straw men. In particular, there runs through portions of the literature the claim that there are internal as well as external explanations of military seizure of power. The internal explanations are those which deal with the nature of military organization; the external, those which deal with the larger political system. I do not know of any empirically oriented study of civil-military relations that would accept or limit itself to one of these approaches. Certainly that was not the strategy of my original essay, which focused on the interplay between military institutions and societal political processes. The crucial issue was and remains that of examining in detail the character of military organization in order to explore the performances of military regimes. In the light of the political developments of 1965 to 1975, the examination has been extended to include the paramilitary and the other police agencies of coercive control. In my original essay, I was concerned with the so-called new nations, the countries of Africa, the Middle East, and Asia that in the main had achieved political independence after 1945; in my reassessment it was necessary to encompass developments in Latin America, since in that region the military has become more "change-oriented."

The "new nations" focus of my original study plus the inclusion of the countries of Latin America encompass the category of "developing nations." I realize well the arbitrary character and limitations of the distinction between industrialized nations and developing nations. The distinction hardly reflects two discrete and mutually exclusive categories, even if one deals with crucial measures of economic institutions, gross national product, and per capita income. But the distinction supplies a continuity with my original analysis as well as a point of departure for the newer efforts.

As a result, I have decided to leave my original essay intact and to augment it with a new one which seeks to deal directly with the role of the paramilitary agencies and their relations to the central armed forces. Both essays appear, therefore, in this edition. I prepared this study explicitly for the Lloyd Fallers memorial seminar. His tragic death deprived me of my essential colleague, the University of Chicago of an effective moral leader, and the social science community of one of its most outstanding minds and a truly international perspective. Since he led me into comparative macrosociology, I would like to think that this essay,

albeit on the ghastly subject of paramilitary forces, can serve as
a tiny memorial.

My knowledge about the developing nations is indeed limited,
and my interest in the topic results from my teaching general
sociology. I have become interested specifically in the role of the
military and paramilitary agencies in these regions because of
my continuing research on the military institutions of the United
States and Western Europe. I would not have been stimulated
to write these essays without the presence of my "comparativist"
colleagues in the Division of the Social Sciences at the University
of Chicago. I could not have written them without their active assistance, direction, and criticism. While they are not responsible
for this "dangerous" effort at a worldwide macrosociology, I
would like to thank Leonard Binder, William Cummings, Philip
Foster, Harry Johnson, Donald Levine, Manning Nash, William
Parish, Philippe Schmitter, Edward Shils, Richard Taub, and
Aristide Zolberg. David Crider assisted effectively in the statistical tabulations. I am particularly grateful for the careful read-
ing of the manuscript by Philippe Schmitter, University of Chicago, and by Charles Moskos, Northwestern University.

The fact that this manuscript was revised and submitted for
publication is due to the stimulus of my colleagues C. I. Eugene
Kim, Western Michigan University, and Charles Moskos, Northwestern University. They prevented it from remaining in the
archives of the Inter-University Seminar on Armed Forces and
Society.

I have carried my assessment and data review to the end of
1975 in order to cover the decade after the original essay. There
is great danger in seeking to be topical in this subject, so the
events since then have not been inserted.

MORRIS JANOWITZ

PREFACE TO THE FIRST EDITION

It can be argued that those nation-states which have come to be called "new nations" do not have enough in common to constitute an appropriate and meaningful group for comparative analysis. This essay proceeds on the counter assumption. There is little purpose in developing a formal definition of a new nation, for the new nations include those countries of Africa and Asia which have achieved independence or have been swept into the process of modernization since the end of World War II. These nations have a unity in the common economic and social problems which they face. Their political institutions have many common features. In particular, these new nations are faced with the paramount task of finding a format for civil-military relations appropriate to their social structure.

The category of new nations is particularly relevant for the comparative analysis of military institutions because of those states which it excludes. Latin American countries, as they seek economic development, have many characteristics comparable to the new nations. Even more pointedly, it appears at first glance that Latin American nations are also confronted with similar crises of civil-military relations. But there are fundamental differences in the natural history of militarism in South America. The forms of military intervention represent more than a century of struggle and accommodation which has produced political institutions different from those found in the new nations. Thus, there is a logic for excluding Latin American nations from this analysis, although the comparative study of the military in politics requires exploration of this particular variant.

This essay focuses on comparative analysis, even though comparison at the nation-state level is an elusive task. The research strategy is to emphasize military institutions and military elites in their common characteristics and in their national differences, in order to throw light on the various patterns of civil-military relations found in new nations. The political sociology of military institutions is a complicated issue. Military institutions and their leaders have a life apart from civil society, although the trend in modern society — both in new nations and in old — is toward a greater penetration of the military into the civilian. "Civilianization" is the other side of the growth in power of the military. But it is only recently that there has been a sustained effort to accumulate materials and to study the organizational behavior of the military in industrialized countries. The available research on the military in new nations, for purposes of comparative analysis, is rather limited. A deeper understanding of military elites in the new nations will require careful and extensive field work, which will often have to be carried out under difficult circumstances.

The justification for this essay, if justification is needed to write on this subject, is that there has been an intellectual imbalance to the study of societal change in new nations. Students of new nations have emphasized economic development, social structure, and political institutions, during a period in which the military has emerged more and more as a crucial institution and power bloc. The specific task of this essay is to sketch a variety of types of civil-military relations in new nations and to formulate a number of hypotheses about the political capacities of the military to rule and to modernize. These conclusions are grounded in the available empirical data.

In a historical sense, it is much too early to evaluate the recent intervention of the military of new nations in domestic politics. But from the point of view of comparative analysis, it is not premature to make a number of generalizations which future research will confirm or refute. This analysis emphasizes the transitional character of the military oligarchies which have emerged since World War II. One of the purposes of comparative analysis is precisely to analyze societal change in such a fashion that the conclusions and hypotheses can in fact be assessed by unfolding events.

A new nation is confronted with the issue of whether the population at large accepts its political leaders as legitimate. New nations are countries where some form of political revolution has taken place. Those which have not had their political revolution are likely to face one. In this process of political revolution, colonial forms are eliminated. The act of national liberation — with or without force — establishes a pragmatic basis for a legitimate government. The military, with its symbols of authority and force, is part of the apparatus of a legitimate government.

But the leaders of new nations, military or civilian, cannot rely exclusively on their revolutionary political activity as a basis for their legitimacy. They hold power in the name of national aspirations for modernization, even though modernization is a means for establishing a national identity and a national sovereignty. In the process of directing societal change, leaders of new nations have a political choice as to the relative balance of coercion versus persuasion that will be used in the efforts to modernize. Paradoxically, this essay on the military is concerned with exploring the extent to which the armed forces can effect change, actually and potentially, in a new nation on the basis of a minimum resort to force and coercion.

M. Janowitz

University of Chicago
September, 1963

I. PARAMILITARY FORCES IN THE DEVELOPING NATIONS

PARAMILITARY FORCES
IN THE DEVELOPING NATIONS

COERCION AND REGIME STABILITY

By case studies and quantitative indicators, the increased participation of military leaders and military groups in the political rule of the developing nations over the fifteen years from 1960 to 1975 has been elaborately recorded. When *The Military in the Political Development of New Nations* was published, the main outline of this worldwide sociopolitical trend had become clear and inescapable.[1] In the ensuing years, there have been individual cases of a return to civilian rule—more often temporary than enduring. But the central tendency has been for the military to exert more influence, either as an active partner in a civilian-military coalition or as a military government. With each increase in their political participation, military institutions have had to make accommodations which in turn have produced some transformation of their organization and practices. As a result, research interest has shifted from a focus on the causes of military intervention to a study of the performance and consequences of military regimes.[2]

[1] Morris Janowitz, *The Military in the Political Development of New Nations: An Essay in Comparative Analysis* (Chicago: University of Chicago Press, 1964); reprinted in this volume. All page references are to this volume.

[2] See for example Philippe C. Schmitter, "Military Intervention: Political Competitiveness and Public Policy in Latin America, 1950–1967," in Morris

3

It was not unanticipated that, with the attenuation and decline of civilian parliamentary rule in the nations that achieved independence after 1945, the personnel of the central military establishment would become active in political leadership. Nor was it unanticipated that the fiscal expenditure for the military establishment in these "new nations" would grow and even be heavy compared with that of an industrialized nation. What was unanticipated was that, in general, the coercion, violence, and repression associated with the initial expansion of the military in the new nations have been relatively limited. In addition, the degree of political stability generated by the initial expansion of the mliitary into domestic politics has also been very limited.[3] In particular instances, charismatic leaders who organized the political movements that resulted in national independence have created the conditions for temporary stability. In nations where the military worked actively to create political coalitions, however, the resulting regimes have hardly been stable or effective. Moreover, where the military assumed direct power, they have not been immune to subsequent coups and continuing political instability. Likewise, the "exit from power" by military groups has generally, with rare exceptions, produced further political instabilities which, in turn, have led to a resumption of military rule.[4]

But the patterns and consequences of military participation have over the years undergone systemic change and transformation—or, at least, that is the argument offered on the basis of an

—————————

Janowitz and Jacques van Doorn, eds., *On Military Intervention* (Rotterdam: Rotterdam University Press, 1971), pp. 425–506.

3 For comparative purposes see W. E. Kaegi, "Patterns of Political Activity of the Armies of the Byzantine Empire," in Janowitz and van Doorn, *On Military Intervention*, pp. 3–36.

4 Henry Bienen and David Morell, eds., "Political Participation under Military Regimes," *Armed Forces and Society: An Interdisciplinary Journal on Military Institutions, Civil-Military Relations, Arms Control and Peacekeeping, and Conflict Management*, vol. 1, special issue (Spring, 1975); Margaret Peil, "A Civilian Appraisal of Military Rule in Nigeria," *Armed Forces and Society* 2 (Fall, 1975):34–35.

assessment of the present state of scholarship and the realities of civil-military relations. In the most succinct terms, the trend has been one which has resulted in increased stability of regimes or, perhaps more accurately, enhanced regime consolidation. There has been a process of "political learning," if you will. Roughly speaking, intense instability occurred in the years from 1945 to 1965, while since 1965 the trend toward more "effective" regimes —that is, more enduring regimes—has become discernible (the supporting data are presented below in table 4). There is no need to exaggerate the extent of this development or to extrapolate it mechanically into the future. The present task is to document and explain the increase in political stability that has frequently been accompanied by an element of domestic political moderation. The dominant perspective in the comparative analysis of the developing nations—both the new nations that have achieved independence since 1945 and those of Latin America—has been a version of economic determinism. There can be no doubt that, to an unspecified extent, increases in political stability and regime durability reflect economic realities, especially the relative amount of economic development linked to the resources extraction that has so dramatically increased monetary flows to a variety of developing nations.

However, my underlying hypothesis moves in a very different direction, for it is concerned with the effects of coercive institutions of these nation-states. Since 1965 one of the noteworthy developments in these nations has been the rapid growth of paramilitary forces that have, over the short run, increased the regimes' stability, that is, their ability to maintain themselves in power. In fact, as documented below, the expansion of paramilitary forces during 1965–75 has been greater than the expansion of the personnel of the central national military establishments.

We are dealing with two differing but converging "natural history" patterns: one in the new nations of Africa, the Middle East, and Asia; the other, in South and Central America. In general, the nations that emerged from colonial domination after 1945 found themselves with very small military institutions and limited paramilitary or police resources; the few where military conflict had been necessary for achieving independence were exceptions. The new nations were incomplete states in the first years after independence; by the standards of the industrialized nations, their apparatus for the monopolization of violence had yet to be developed. The outstanding characteristic of the military leaders of these new nations, compared to the patterns of the nation-states of Western Europe, was the extent to which they professed a commitment to sociopolitical change. They were prepared to assume political power, in varying degrees, in the name of such change.

By contrast, military leaders in Latin American nations were, in general, until the early 1960s, crucial in regulating factional disputes among existing elite groups. They served as active elements in maintaining a political balance or stable imbalance. But the perspective of the military in South America—and, in particular cases, in Central America—has been converging with that of the new nations. These military establishments have become more involved, seeking to direct and arbitrate sociopolitical change. The self-imposed tasks of these military establishments and their paramilitary agencies have thus become enlarged and intensified.

Because the literature of sociopolitical change in the new nations and in Latin America has focused on the national military establishment, it has not encompassed the full realities of coercive control. The day-to-day patterns of control rest to an important degree on the variety of police and paramilitary that symbolize the extent of the governments' penetration to the local levels— urban and rural. Thus it is necessary to examine in detail the expansion of the paramilitary forces in the developing nations, especially during 1965–75. In general, the increased capacity of the regimes in these nations to rule has been a function of institution building, and especially of the increased growth and effectiveness of their police agencies—those instruments of repressive control. In the process of institution building, one important feature has been the extension of direction and control of the police and the paramilitary by the central national military establishment.

The size of paramilitary units does not in itself determine their actual and potential function and influence. Size is but an important measure or indicator of institutional change. It is the structure of these organizations and the functions they perform that are important. Thus the impact of the paramilitary forces reflects the goals, aspirations, and organizational effectiveness of the elites who manage them. In essence the underlying issue is the persistence—and, in effect, the increased effectiveness—of authoritarian rule in the developing nations; and to investigate this, we must examine the paramilitary forces.

Of course, the growth of the paramilitary forces in the developing nations has, since World War II, taken place in the context of rapid population growth and extensive urbanization. Thus the paramilitary forces have in part grown as a result of the increasing necessity to police urban areas and to control "ordinary" crime. Paramilitary forces play a role in this type of local policing. However, they have not been expanded primarily to deal with nonpolitical crime. It must be recognized, moreover, that the paramilitary forces, as do other types of government employment, provide a base for political patronage and reward—another reason for their expansion. Nevertheless, the argument that will be explored is that their expansion contributes to regime stability because of the increased resources at the disposal of the groups in power.

It must be emphasized that in general we are dealing with a reactive trend; that is, the increased emphasis and reliance on coercive agencies are not, initially or primarily, the result of a grand design or explicit intention. Instead, the absence of or the failure to develop more effective patterns of political and social control leads military regimes or military-based regimes to rely more heavily on internal police control.

In this connection, the scope and content of elite goals—political, economic, and social—are crucial components of the degree of regime stability. One cannot escape the intriguing idea that, in the decade from 1965 to 1975, the increase in regime stability has reflected growing moderation in elite goals and aspirations. Overreaching goals contribute to political instability, while more realistic goals are less disruptive. More realistic societal goals imply that the available coercive resources are likely to be more effective.

The formation and advocacy of national goals are not a series of random processes. They appear and are transformed with a considerable amount of uniformity. From the very beginning of my reassessment, I have been struck by a common pattern. Without overstating the case, I shall seek to describe the extent to which the simple, and in a real sense oversimplified, idea of the "natural history of revolution," or, as I prefer, the "natural history of societal transformation," is applicable to the recent history of the developing nations.

Thus, I shall proceed with two interlocking hypotheses as partial but relevant explanations of the pattern of regime consolidation in the developing nations during the decade 1965–75. First, this pattern is a function in part of the greater size and effectiveness of paramilitary forces that increase the ability of political regimes to maintain their power. Second, the pattern is a function of the transformation of elite goals and aspirations that, following a "natural history," have become more circumscribed and more moderate, and thus more realistic.

This perspective was originally presented after World War I by Lyford P. Edwards and Crane Brinton.[5] These early efforts at analytic history did not lose the historical realities. These authors had no single-factor theory of sociopolitical change; nor did they believe in overdetermined models—patterns and cycles of revo-

[5] Lyford P. Edwards, *The Natural History of Revolution* (Chicago: University of Chicago Press, 1927); Crane Brinton, *The Anatomy of Revolution* (New York: Norton, 1938).

lution. However, they noted a series of regularities in revolutions: the initial period of discontent; the first phase of limited change; the subsequent emergence of extreme revolutionary or militant aspirations and efforts; and, in time, the development of a period of relative moderation and consolidation—a Thermidor, if you will. As one traces them case by case after 1945, one sees in the military regimes and their performance—or lack of performance—repeated parallels to this natural history.

Growing political participation by military groups in the developing nations does not mean the end of civilian interest groups or of interest-group politics. In addition, the military regimes struggle to develop an effective articulation with the civilian bureaucratic agencies. The increased participation of military groups in the political process does mean that there is a new balance between persuasion and coercion.

Our orientation is of course worldwide, for that is the style of comparative macrosociology. But we shall proceed on a country-by-country basis, and by regional comparisons, since geographic and historical and cultural parameters cannot be disregarded for a moment—they give substantive meaning to the broad generalization about the importance of the agencies of internal coercion.

PERSPECTIVES ON CIVIL-MILITARY RELATIONS

There is no need to dwell on the ideological and academic barriers to the study of military institutions and of the role of coercion in sociopolitical change. These have been extensively debated. However, it is important to reassert that the subject by its very nature does not lend itself readily to intellectualization. (The analysis of economic behavior—with its assumption of human rationality—is a more fitting and productive topic of social research.) Of course, it is necessary to explore the topic of the military in developing nations with a great deal of detachment and self-criticism, but without the intellectual posture of callous scientism, on the one hand, or of romantic rationalism—reactionary or radical—on the other.[6] The intellectual capital that we have accumulated is indeed limited. More often than not, it undermines simplified notions and mechanical formulations.

Any assessment of the progress and present state of scholarship about the developing nations must immediately address three questions concerning the military, although these questions are of declining importance. First, has there been sufficient emphasis on the role of military institutions in the three decades since decolonization started after World War II? Second, have the efforts at comparative analysis of "armed forces and society" been pursued in sufficiently comprehensive terms? Third, how clarifying has the literature been in assessing the influence of coercion in sociopolitical change and regime consolidation?

Obviously, the first question—whether there has been adequate emphasis on the social and political roles of the military—invites a negative answer. Such a response reflects the traditions of Western scholarship, in which there has been a long-standing neglect of the linkages between military institutions and the macrosociology of political regimes. I am not overlooking the enormous literature devoted to the strategic analysis of international relations. But the fundamental character of Western macropolitical sociology and political science analysis can best be judged in the format in which the history of Western nation-states—nation building in Western Europe and the United States—is basically written: in terms of the extension of the franchise. The profound impact of war and the complex role of military institutions in the emergence of parliamentary institutions are only slowly being brought into focus. In other words, the investigation of the developing nations by Western scholars predictably has been an extension and modification of their intellectual analysis of Western institutions and the process of sociopolitical change in the West.

The perspectives of the particular scholars who have become involved in the analysis of nation building in Asia, the Middle

[6] Morris Janowitz, "International Perspectives on Militarism," *American Sociologist* 3 (February 1968): 12–16.

East, and Africa have only reinforced such orientations. Economists have perceived military institutions as essential fixed costs and potential burdens on economic development budgets. Most anthropologists and sociologists active in field research have had expertise in community studies. They have emphasized languages and social and cultural history rather than the analysis of a societal perspective and the particular effect of military institutions.

However, in a very fundamental sense, this type of assessment is incomplete and, perhaps more to the point, irrelevant. In retrospect—and without our commenting on the quality of their research efforts—it seems that scholars, in their effort to construct a macropolitical sociology, have perhaps emphasized military institutions in the developing nations to a comparatively greater extent than they have in the Western nation-state.

The role of the military in the political development of new nations has quickly become a matter of academic interest and debate, if not of intensive scholarship. Very rapidly, the breakdown of parliamentary institutions in specific new nations, plus the backdrop of a century of military intervention in Latin America, have made researchers aware of the subject of armed forces and society. The heritage of Turkey under Ataturk also serves as a focal point for intellectual formulations.[7] The policy issues of military assistance and the basic issues of political strategies of social and economic development have produced academic pronouncements, couched in the language of social research, that have been mainly polemical. Most of these "models of the emerging future" have grossly exaggerated the capacities of the military as "agents of modernization," but a minority have been essentially correct.[8]

The early (until 1965) phase of interest in the military in the new nations produced a series of speculative essays—exercises in

[7] Bernard Lewis, *The Emergence of Modern Turkey* (London: Oxford University Press, 1961).

[8] For an emphasis on military potentials for political and economic stability, see Guy J. Pauker, "Southeast Asia as a Problem Area in the Next Decade," *World Politics* 11 (April 1959): 325–45.

comparative analysis. There can be no doubt that much of the writing of this period has disappeared with appropriate dispatch. The lasting contribution of these efforts was their emphasis on the restrictions and difficulties that military regimes would confront in their attempts to achieve economic development and political stability. They focused on the inherent tendencies of military regimes to fragment and to experience countercoups. The early writings asserted that military elites could not serve as agents of development because they were intrinsically unable fully to perpetuate and generate their political legitimacy and to produce some form of effective mass political participation. Clearly, as we can see in retrospect, the most salient formulation of these essays was that military regimes, to be effective agents of sociopolitical change, had to accomplish joint and mutually reinforcing objectives. They had to maintain their own internal cohesion; on the other hand, they had consciously to limit their direct involvement in the political process. This limitation could be achieved if a charismatic leader arose or if the military regime used a political formula to mobilize or create civilian groups through which it could exercise and share political power. The early essays also stimulated a growing number of comprehensive case studies that in turn have prepared the groundwork for a contemporary reassessment of the military and coercion in the developing nations.

But the scholarly concern with military institutions must be seen in terms of the problems of intellectual "logistics." After 1945 most of the effective scholarship on the new nations focused on institutional arrangements grounded in the indigenous environment and continuity—for example, village structure, religious institutions, and the like. The political parties were relatively new institutions, but political forms had more continuity with the colonial period than was found in the military establishment. The military institutions—in sheer expansion—were truly the new institutions of the developing nations. In essence, time had to elapse before there was a phenomenon that could be analyzed in depth—before the military institutions' influence, or lack of influence, on social structure and social organization could be observed and assessed. In fact, scholars plunged in without reserve or academic discretion to identify the variables that accounted for military groups' expansion and seizure of political power. Since this process was very generalized, the underlying problem was to account for the examples that did not conform to the historical pattern. Only slowly was the central issue redefined to that of the varying performances of military regimes.

The second question deals with the scope of comparative analysis of military institutions in the developing nations. The diversity in size of these nations presents formidable barriers to comparative analysis, as do the complexities of cultural, ethnic, linguistic, and, of course, economic differences. But the strong element of uniformity in military organization has contributed to a continually widening perspective for comparative analysis.

Military institutions of the developing nations have been based on the wholesale transplantation of Western military technology and, in varying degrees, of Western organizational format. Comparative analysis has meant to contrast the military institutions of different classes of developing nations with each other and with those of the industrialized nations—more often with those of the Western parliamentary nations than with those of the East European single mass-party systems. The logic of investigation generally has involved a fusion of two sets of variables. On the one hand, there are the dimensions of the military organization and the military profession that reflect the relative standardization of classes of military technology and military organization. On the other hand, there are the dimensions that deal with the wide differences in patterns of social recruitment and socialization into the military profession as well as differences in the cultural context.

But comparative analysis of military institutions in the new nations is not based solely on analytical considerations. The exciting drama of the end of colonialism after World War II created a class of nation-states with a commonality rooted in their contemporary history. The idea of the developing nations is a worldwide formula based on economic measures. But the term "new nations" is a historical designation for those political entities that achieved their independence or disengaged themselves from the influence of European colonial rule in the years immediately after World War II. With exceptions, their independence came with little violence or warfare. This commonality has supplied an important basis for comparative analysis. In varying degrees, this commonality has involved a divergence, in the institutional perspective of the military elites of the new nations, from that which had been operative in Western military formations derived from European feudalism and nineteenth-century professionalism.[9] Students of macrosociology have been confronted with the imagery and the corresponding reality of a military establishment that has an enunciated commitment to managed and contrived sociopolitical change rather than to an overwhelming acceptance of the status quo—the conservative essence of Western military institutions.

For this reason, in the 1950s and earlier 1960s, in the comparative analysis of the developing nations, a meaningful distinction could be made between the new nations of Africa, the Middle East, and Asia, on the one hand, and the nations of Latin America, on the other. However, the military in Latin America was different. In Latin America, the movement toward independence had taken place a century earlier and had involved extensive violence and warfare. The military institutions of Latin America evolved into institutions that were analogous to the sociopolitical format of Western Europe. The military emerged with an institutional perspective that was conservative and accepted the status quo. After World War I, the Latin American military forces started

    [9] John J. Johnson, ed., *The Role of the Military in Underdeveloped Countries* (Princeton, N.J.: Princeton University Press, 1962); Edward A. Shils, *The Political Development in the New States* (The Hague: Mouton, 1965), pp. 44–45; Karl Demeter, *Das Deutsche Heer und seine Offiziere* (Berlin: Verlag von Reimar, 1935); for an analysis of the emergence of military professionalism from mercenary formations, see Maury Feld, "Middle-Class Society and the Rise of Military Professionalism: The Dutch Army, 1589–1609," *Armed Forces and Society* 1 (Summer 1975): 419–42.

to change in recruitment and professionalization. The organization format they developed included limited accommodation to sociopolitical change. In particular instances, it sought to respond to the demands of an enlarged middle-class stratum; and at the turn of the century there were Latin American countries whose military had strong "progressive" components. But the essential pattern was the military's commitment to maintaining the status quo. In the 1960s gradual changes occurred with elements of an interesting convergence—if one wishes to use the term. In increasing numbers, the military elites of Latin America, because of shifting patterns of social recruitment, new forms of professionalization, and domestic political agitations, began to converge with the military formations of the new nations. They developed a stronger and more explicit orientation toward sociopolitical change, in part repeating earlier abortive attempts. As a result, there was a redefinition of government's role and potentials for achieving economic development and "social justice." Thus, in assessing the strategies of crossnational comparison of the role of the military in the political development of developing nations since World War II, we must use a perspective that encompasses Latin America.

The dominant characteristic of the military in the context of contemporary nationalism is that it is an indivisible entity. In any given territory, to have a legitimate government means to have a single coherent armed force. In the postcolonial period of world history, the members of the military are not organized and defined as mercenaries or as personal vassals of competing political leaders. They are organized and defined as forming an agency of the national state—that is, as an official bureaucracy. The military operates as a form of public service, if the term is used in its broadest connotation to emphasize secular and national dimensions.

But the third question is central in reassessing scholarship about the developing nations. Was the analysis of military institutions pursued in terms that helped clarify the realities of coercion as an instrument of sociopolitical stability or change in the developing nations? Scholarship focused on the national military forces, since these institutions encompassed the preponderant potentials for political coercion. However, the imagery and definition that researchers held of these formations—and I include my own— were not sufficiently accurate or realistic. In essence, the military establishment was seen in rather circumscribed, formal, and delimited terms—mainly as the locus for recruiting political and administrative leaders and subleaders.

The military institutions were not effectively used as the point of departure for the study of the actual patterns of coercion. We studied the formal structure and certain limited aspects of the operations of national armed forces. But we did not realistically use Harold D. Lasswell's formulation and respond to the need to study management of the instruments of violence, a much broader and more generic topic.[10] Of course, I was fully aware that, in the developing nations, there existed national and local police forces, national security services, political police, domestic intelligence services, and a variety of paramilitary units (full-time and part-time) plus various combinations of thugs. There were comprehensive systems of courts and prisons as well. But data about these formations are not easily collected, and in the study of the new nations, collecting them was politically sensitive. In macro-

---

[10] For an exploration of sociopolitical processes which resulted in civilian control and paramilitary democracy in Western European states, see Morris Janowitz, "Military Institutions and Citizenship in Western Societies," *Armed Forces and Society* 2 (Winter 1976): 185–204; see also Samuel E. Finer, "State and Nation Building in Europe: The Role of the Military," in *The Formation of National States in Western Europe* (Princeton, N.J.: Princeton University Press, 1975), pp. 84–163; Harold D. Lasswell, *Politics: Who Gets What, When, How* (Glencoe, Ill.: Free Press, 1951); Harold D. Lasswell, "The Garrison State," *American Journal of Sociology* 46 (January 1941): 455–68. In his original formulation of the "garrison state," Lasswell focused on the expansion of the role of the armed forces (see Lasswell, "Garrison State"). In a reformulation and elaboration of the concept a decade later, he gave increasing importance to the police and paramilitary formations as elements of the garrsion state: see Harold D. Lasswell, "The Garrison State Hypothesis Today," in Samuel Huntington, ed., *Changing Patterns of Military Politics* (Glencoe, Ill.: Free Press, 1962), pp. 51–70.

sociology, naturalistic categories about violence have never been in good standing; they have traditionally been criticized as a subtle or not so subtle form of ideological support for authoritarian political practices. Moreover, there are no great theories of violence, as there are theories of social stratification and culture.

Nevertheless, I am convinced that military and paramilitary institutions operate with different organizational logic than other institutional sectors. It is particularly relevant that military personnel bring a specialized perspective and specialized skills to the political process, although this observation is fully compatible with the idea that persons who ascend to the highest leadership positions of a society accumulate common political skills that transcend their functional specialization.

Military institutions in the developing nations are very visible and dramatic. Despite secrecy, it has been possible to observe the main outlines of the military in domestic affairs. In particular, the role of the military in recruiting top political and administrative elites has been immediately discernible—in fact, unavoidable. But tracing the linkages of the national military establishment to the paramilitary and police agencies has presented a different and more difficult set of research tasks. I was impressed by the fact that from 1945 to 1965 national and local police forces played a minor or very infrequently active role in the expansion of political power by the regular armed forces. To be sure, the organizational weight of the central armed forces was critical in shifting the composition and coalitions of the elites. However, I failed to recognize adequately that the expansion of the political activity of the national military formation rested on and was facilitated by the internal paramilitary police control system. Even without active conspiracy or collaboration, the national military forces were able to seize and exercise power because they could assume that they had the tacit support of the existing police and paramilitary forces. The latter, in turn, were able to exercise sufficient control to permit the military to restructure the regimes without extensive violence. Although police and paramilitary units were limited and continued to grow with time, they were crucial in the day-to-day maintenance of internal order.

In part, popular opposition was low or inhibited. There were persistent public protests and mass demonstrations in certain nations, but the level of discontent must be judged as fairly contained and not easily exploited by a counterelite. In retrospect, however, I judge that my analysis of military intervention in political power during the first years after 1945 was incomplete, since it did not encompass the actual, although latent, forms of support the military had from the other internal coercive agencies.

After 1965 the level of violence by ruling groups against unorganized, quasi-organized, or organized opposition elements seems to have increased to some degree. This is at best an impression, and careful scholarship will be required to document and explicate it. When I wrote *The Military in the Political Development of New Nations,* I should have known that there was no reason to believe that the existing patterns of military intervention with limited violence would continue. It is true that I spoke of the limits of military rule and said that, if it did not develop an important component of civilianization, it "will not be conducive to an orderly and humane process of modernization."[11]

At the time, I had every reason to believe that increased coercion was probable. The obvious fragmentation of the military frequently required competing factions to mobilize external support and to engage in repressive measures to maintain their ascendancy. In extreme situations, the result was "organized" civil war, as in Nigeria and Indonesia, with extensive human cost. Equally destructive was informal civil war—against particular tribal and ethnic groups, as in the Sudan, Chad, and Iraq. More persistent was the extension of day-to-day repressive techniques of control, including expulsion of minority groups, that became more and more 'pervasive and widespread. Likewise, factional struggles among the military occurred in the context of higher levels of popular discontent. While it is hardly appropriate to speak of

[11] See below, p. 182.

mass mobilization, we can say that the achievement of political independence did politicalize particular groups in society. Perhaps it would be more accurate to say that after 1965 military regimes have had to confront more effectively organized counterelites; as a result, their coercive practices have increased.

Interestingly enough, since 1945 the frequency and scope of conventional international warfare among the developing nations, with the exception of the combined-Arab-Israeli conflict, have remained low by historical standards. The major international war has been the India-Pakistan engagements, which may, however, be considered a form of postcolonial civil war. In fact, we are dealing with a historical epoch in which the distinction between civil war and international warfare is either arbitrary or derived from colonial experiences.

My underestimation of the role of paramilitary and police agencies in the internal coercion of the developing nations seems to have been caused by two factors. The first, and probably minor or peripheral, cause was reverse prejudice. The attraction, almost veneration, which many scholars felt for the new nations probably inhibited my exploration of the realities of these institutions. Second, the literature on the institutions of the new nations, in particular on their political institutions, served in a way to mislead me.

The dominant theme before 1965 was that the new nations were being "mobilized" by their political institutions. The social structures of these societies were being fundamentally transformed because of enlarged political participation. Clearly, there was little basis for such a view; the members of the University of Chicago's Committee for the Comparative Study of New Nations were correct in criticizing it. However, as a result of their counterformulations, I tended to underemphasize the potential for partial growth of effectiveness of the military and related institutions of these nations.[12]

[12] In part, my perspective was distorted as a result of my limited review of the intelligence services, the internal security apparatus, and the external subversion exercises of certain new nations. In the early 1960s the ineffec-

Thus, the period since 1965 has seen increases in the capacity for internal coercion and in coercive practices in the developing nations—both in the new nations and in Latin America. My reassessment is that coercive practices have not only become more frequent and widespread but have also frequently emerged as more effective ways to consolidate and maintain regime stability. In short, the elites—especially those recruited from the military—have built more viable instruments through which to exercise their power more effectively.

The role of coercion in the developing nations requires a perspective that encompasses more than the military, one that can include coercive institutions, such as police and paramilitary formations, and the various forms of repression. The relative absence of coercion in the initial seizure of power gives way to more reliance on "systemic" coercive control to maintain power. However, it must be continually emphasized that these levels hardly approximate those of totalitarian regimes.

Military regimes and regimes dependent on military forces do not operate through the exercise of day-to-day techniques of internal control by the military institutions. Not only do the military regimes take the local police and paramilitary formations for granted, but they also seek to fashion and direct them. Though military regimes and professional officers resist the direct exercise of the police function, they recognize that political power rests in part on the performance of such a function by a "lower order" of agents.

Most scholars engaged in studying the developing nations focus on the barriers—economic, social, and cultural—to development or on the special conditions under which economic growth takes place. But a perspective on institution building indicates that a regime's capacity to govern—as shown by its ability to consolidate power and to remain in power—is related more to its institution-

tiveness of these services was most conspicuous, highlighted and compounded in various instances by the limited results of foreign assistance in these arenas.

building capacities, at whose center is its internal security and coercive system. To speak of increased regime stability, grounded or assisted by more effective internal security systems, is not to disregard the vulnerabilities of authoritarian regimes, particularly the crisis linked to leadership succession.

The sociopolitical movements of the developing nations are responses to both internal and external circumstances. We must always remember that all nation-states do not have the same potentials for social transformation—a simple observation all too often neglected in present comparative macrosociology. Natural resources, size, and geopolitical location are all crucial but underacknowledged variables. Moreover, there is no reason to proceed as if each nation-state were a separate and independent object of analysis, as much of aggregate data research does. Developing nations are subject in different degrees to external penetration; and even more to the point, each has a series of international linkages and is therefore responding to powerful processes of regional diffusion, especially in its management of the agencies of national defense and internal coercion. A nation's military leaders are self-conscious men who come to recognize that the fate of their nation is related to regional and international developments.

The core issues are not theoretical or methodological but factual. This essay suffers from a lack of data and the degree of my ability to assimilate that documentation which is available. On the positive side, there is a body of documentary materials that enables one to present some revealing indicators of the growth of the military and paramilitary agencies of the developing nations on a comparative and trend basis. On the negative side, the number and range of detailed monographic studies are limited but growing; in particular, there is almost no research on the perspective of military leaders. Social scientists have not involved themselves much in this topic. Research of this type has inherent and growing difficulties. But this essay has been made possible because there are, on the campus of the University of Chicago, a group of social science specialists—regional and comparative specialists—

who have been my academic informants and have supplied me with essential assessments and explications and provided the context for interpreting the available data.

MILITARY ELITES AND POLITICS

The propositions and generalizations about the political behavior of military (and, by extension, paramilitary) leaders that have been entered into the literature must be used with extreme caution. For example, Samuel Huntington uses his empirical investigations to conclude that the professionalization of military men contributes to and in fact ensures their political neutrality.[13] If one uses, as criteria for professionalization, technical expertise, group cohesion, and an important amount of self-regulation, there is no reason, as Bengt Abrahamsson and others have pointed out, to argue that this observation applies to the industrialized nations of the world community, and even less reason to believe that it holds for the developing nations.[14] From the viewpoint of Huntington's political philosophy, it would be desirable if military professionalism included a normative code of political neutrality. However, this is an incomplete statement and a weak use of the term "political neutrality," because democratic theory requires that military professionals be neutral—that is, not politically partisan—but nevertheless fully committed to the rules of the political process. Moreover, at this point Huntington's analysis becomes mainly a discourse in political philosophy, since he asserts—and in fact desires—that the military profession, by virtue of its recruitment, socialization, and professional requirements, will emerge with a uniform orientation and that this orientation will in effect be conservative. Again, such a conclusion bears little relation to the realities of industrialized nations and has no meaning for the developing nations, whose military can hardly be described as conservative.

[13] Samuel P. Huntington, *Political Order in Changing Societies* (New Haven: Yale University Press, 1968).
[14] Bengt Abrahamsson, *Military Professionalism and Political Power* (Beverly Hills, Calif.: Sage Publications, 1972).

In his analysis of the political behavior of the military professionals, Huntington asserts that there are two different types of explanation of military intervention in national politics. He claims that one set of explanations is rooted in the characteristics of military organization; the second set, in the "political institutional structure of the society." Huntington rejects the first and accepts the second.[15] But it is impossible to locate those scholars who put forth the first claim. Those, including myself, who have been concerned with the nature of military rule and the military's capacities to rule have asserted that military intervention in the developing nations after 1945 generally has occurred after the existing political system has weakened or collapsed, especially in the wake of a disarray of parliamentary institutions.[16] The distinction Huntington offers is without merit, since in fact the role of the military in the developing nations—and in the industrialized nations as well—is the result of a process of interaction; that is, it reflects the interplay of the political order, with its strains and difficulties, and the institutional and occupational characteristics of the military. With this perspctive, we return again and again to the more central, the more essential issue, namely, the manner in which military coalitions and military regimes organize politics and the performance of their regimes under the pressures of exercising power.

Huntington and others have dealt with the issue of performance mainly in terms of the ability or inability of a regime to produce economic development and increased expenditure for social welfare. An assessment of their efforts demonstrates the extent to which the literature has produced negative findings; but negative findings have merit.[17]

[15] Huntington, *Political Order*, pp. 193–94.
[16] See below, pp. 80–106.
[17] Schmitter, "Military Intervention"; Robert W. Jackman, "Politicians in Uniform: Military Governments and Social Change in the Third World," *American Political Science Review* 70 (December 1976); Jerry L. Weaver, "Assessing the Impact of Military Rule: Alternative Approaches," in Philippe Schmitter, ed., *Military Rule in Latin America: Function, Consequences, and Perspectives* (Beverly Hills, Calif.: Sage Publications, 1973), pp. 58–116.

The ground has effectively been cleared of those who, soon after 1950, stressed the potentialities of military leadership for economic development; it has likewise been cleared of those who emphasized the military's inability to produce economic development. If one had to choose between these formulations, the alternative that underlines the limitations of the military appears much sounder. But such a choice has never been required. The argument never seems fruitful, since it has failed to take into consideration variations in natural resources and ecological structure—and, most important, to specify the political conditions under which military regimes could produce economic and social development.

The results of quantitative research on the ability of military regimes to produce economic growth are as might have been anticipated; there is no reason to conclude that military regimes are more or less successful than civilian regimes in producing economic development. On a case-by-case analysis, one can find particular military regimes that are among those with the highest rates of economic development, but viewed overall, military regimes do not produce higher rates of economic growth.

Quantitative studies on military regimes and economic development are, of course, fraught with technical problems.[18] There is the matter of the adequacy, validity, and relevance of the basic data about economic growth. There is the even more difficult task of categorizing the form and extent of military government. Research strategy tends to reify the process of military intervention, to create a set of traits and rather fixed categories when, in effect, we are dealing with a complex, almost stochastic process in which

[18] Robert D. Putnam, "Toward Explaining Military Intervention in Latin America," *World Politics* 20 (October 1967): 83–110; Irma Adelman and Cynthia T. Morris, *Society, Politics, and Economic Development: A Quantitative Approach* (Baltimore: Johns Hopkins University Press, 1967); Douglas P. Bury, "Political Instability in Latin America: The Cross-Cultural Test of a Causal Model," *Latin American Research Review* 3 (1968): 17–66; Eric A. Nordlinger, "Soldiers in Mufti: The Impact of Military Rule upon Economic and Social Change in the Non-Western States," *American Political Science Review* 64 (December 1970): 1131–48.

the universe has been drifting toward increased military intervention. Moreover, it is essential to determine the appropriate mode of statistical analysis when the size of the universe is limited and the data hardly meet standard statistical requirements.[19]

But one cannot overlook the weight of the negative findings, since they articulate with common sense. In short, some military regimes produce economic development, others do not. Moreover, effective multivariate analysis would require a frame of reference more profound than that based on the variables included in the available statistical analysis. As a result, the long-standing question is more relevant and more manageable for the task at hand: what are the institutional and political adaptations which occur under military rule as a result of the efforts of the military regimes to consolidate their power? The original formulation I offered focused on whether military regimes could "help create some of the mass apparatus which makes possible the shaping of a minimum level of political consensus." Either the military would have to create such an apparatus or it would have to assist civilian groups to create appropriate agencies. Although they have made various efforts with some persistent results, military regimes have not been conspicuously successful in attaining

---

[19] One of the striking aspects of this literature is its intensive concern with the appropriate strategy of statistical and mathematical analysis rather than with the quality, validity, and categorization of the data. As a result, one must, on the whole, assess and utilize the findings with reservations, except, as indicated above, where they emphasize negative conclusions that thereby prevent oversimplified formulations from being accepted as "reality." Even in their own terms the methodologies do not articulate effectively with the requirements of hypothesis testing by quantitative procedures. Thus the statistical procedures employed are often more useful for descriptive purposes as data-reduction techniques rather than as procedures for testing and evaluating hypotheses. This is particularly true when factor analysis is applied, and often when path analysis is applied, especially where cross-sectional data are utilized. Tests of hypotheses by regression techniques and so-called causal models often rely on data that do not meet the statistical assumptions and requirements. This is not to assert that the task is essentially unproductive or without promise. There is reason to believe that statistical strategies such as Leo Goodman's semi-log techniques, which I have found more appropriate for macrosociological data, may well be applied to cross-sectional national data with more than negative results.

this goal. Instead, they have turned their attention to fashioning and expanding police and paramilitary agencies as agents of political power.

TRENDS IN MILITARY AND PARAMILITARY FORCES

Thus our initial task is to chart the trends in military and paramilitary manpower from 1965 to 1975 in order to explore the changing morphology of the instruments for monopolizing coercion. The data will enable us to examine the noteworthy expansion of paramilitary forces. This task is rewarding in that it permits and requires one to be fully candid about the quality and limitations of the data one is collecting and using and thereby to avoid the mechanistic and excessively reified approach to quantitative cross-national research.

To assemble and organize these trend indicators, we followed certain steps. First, we collected data worldwide, so that we could make some comparisons between industrialized nations and developing nations. We sought to focus on the extent to which paramilitary institutions in the new nations and in Latin America have expanded, especially since 1965. In doing so, we had to probe the trends of military and paramilitary institutions in the industrialized nations of the West as well as of the one-party states of Eastern Europe.

Second, we had to determine the accuracy and validity of trend data and we had to establish a relevant categorization, since, over the world, the types of paramilitary and police forces present truly bewildering variations. While resources and attempts to collect these data have grown enormously during the last decade, limitations and defects should not be overlooked. There can be no doubt that the interest of scholars has stimulated an improved data basis. Since my initial interest in these matters in the early 1960s, I have found that the Research Committee on Armed Forces and Society of the International Sociological Association has supplied an international focal point for data collection. The handbook of social and political indicators published in the

United States tends to deemphasize the tasks of assessment and evaluation of data from public sources.[20] However, over the years, the International Institute of Strategic Studies, London, has become a central repository of fairly accurate worldwide data, not only on military forces but also on paramilitary and national police forces. Data on local police are much more scanty.

The basic categorization has had to be developed in a comparable and standardized rubric that would permit classification in terms of the distinction between the central military forces and the paramilitary and national police forces. Local police personnel are excluded from our morphology. However, we have had to include data on part-time armed military groups because of their internal security function. These data are based on official statistics of the governments involved, journalists' reports, and Western government sources—mainly and most importantly British sources. I have sought to augment these data by information from United States sources and informants around the world. In the process, we should emphasize, important variations have been encountered that reflect the limitations of the data and inhibit inference and analysis. My approach has been, not to average out inconsistent and contradictory reports, but rather, on the basis of internal evidence, to make the best estimate.

Although the categorization is not without some ambiguity, it is possible to organize the data in a worldwide system that highlights the distinctions among the active duty military force, the reserve military force, the national police force, and the paramilitary units, and which excludes the local police. Further refinement is required as defined below:

I. *Regular Military Forces*

1. Active Duty Military Forces—Full-time army, navy, and air force formations under the direct control and organiza-

[20] Arthur S. Banks and Robert B. Textor, *A Cross-Polity Survey* (Cambridge: MIT Press, 1963); Arthur S. Banks, *Cross-Polity Time Series Data* (Cambridge: MIT Press, 1971); Charles L. Taylor and Michael C. Hudson, *World Handbook of Political and Social Indicators* (New Haven: Yale University Press, 1972).

tion of the central government. Personnel may be volunteer or conscripted.

2. Reserve Forces

   A. Standby—Army, navy, and air force personnel, under the direct control and organization of the central government, who can be mobilized rapidly in periods of tension and conflict and who are part of the operational military.

   B. Organized—Army, navy, and air force personnel, under the direct control and organization of the central government, whose effective mobilization and integration require longer periods than those required for standby forces.

   C. Militia—An aspect of the central military force and used as a reserve for national defense purposes. Personnel are fully uniformed and available for mobilization assignments in regular national defense forces.

II. *Paramilitary Units*

   3. National Police Force—Full-time "militarized" police units, domiciled in part in barracks, equipped with light military weapons and military vehicles, and organized under the central government. Includes frontier guard units. Often called gendarmerie.

   4. Local Defense Units—Armed local personnel, domiciled at home, typically without or with only partial uniforms, and deployed in their own area. Essentially part-time military defense units in connection with internal armed insurrections. In some developing countries, called militia.

   5. Workers' Militia—Part-time personnel recruited on the basis of criteria of political reliability. Industrialized societies' equivalent of local defense units designed mainly for domestic security; mobilized in ceremonial and politically critical situations. Domiciled at home. Partially uniformed and only partially armed, but can include units with military reserve functions.

III. Local Police

> 6. Local Police Formations—Full-time, uniformed police, domiciled in their homes, without military weapons. Involved in day-to-day local police functions, and in riot control and certain internal security tasks.

Using these categories, we have been able to define paramilitary forces meaningfully and to tabulate trends in size (table 1, p. 36). For worldwide comparability, we have defined "paramilitary forces" as essentially including the different types of national police forces and those militia personnel who have internal security functions. As mentioned, local police forces have not been tabulated. Other types of paramilitary and police forces could not be integrated into the data-collection scheme. There are, especially in developing nations, a variety of irregular forces in addition to local defense units, but their number and scope are declining. Of crucial importance are the political police or "security police"—both uniformed and ununiformed—and their networks of countless agents. These groups are organized in various fashions, sometimes under the ministry of interior, sometimes under the military, sometimes as an independent group, or in different combinations. Most nations have more than one security agency, and the agencies compete with each other. There are nations where the military intelligence units also function as political police. Quantitative data about political police are scanty and unreliable, and numerical strength does not necessarily or pertinently indicate the role political police have in the system of coercion. Moreover, the police make extensive use of part-time personnel who work for money or political favors or because of pressure. Official budgets for both the military and the paramilitary are hardly revealing indicators, since important items are "buried" in other agencies, mislabeled, or just unreported. But whatever the level of economic development, there are generous budgets for the political police, who engage in surveillance, intimidation and direct coercion, physical control and detention, and the endless variety of manipulative devices that centuries of human exploitation have developed.

For statistical tabulation, we have eliminated those nations with populations of fewer than one million. Their tragic circumstances—with one or two exceptions—render them less than real wholes. The typical developing nation is relatively small—two to eight million. But the few very large developing nations have a large proportion of the total population of the developing nations; these must be perceived as a distinct group. Later, these statistical arrays are presented in detail.

The transformation in the morphology of the institutions of coercive control in the developing nations encompasses more than an expansion of the paramilitary and national police forces and the undocumented growth of the secret and political police. The crux of the analysis rests on the articulation of control of the paramilitary forces by the national military establishment and by the politicalized elements of the military who are involved in the political regime.

In Western industrialized nations with parliamentary regimes, the institutional separation of the forces of national defense from the agencies of internal policing is considered vital for the maintenance of a democratic policy and a competitive electoral system. In the developing nations, this separation is less in demand—and frequently missing.

As of 1975, there are a few "traditional" personal authoritarian regimes, as in Saudi Arabia, where the ruler seeks to maintain a balance of power between the paramilitary units and the national military establishment in order to strengthen his regime. However, such arrangements are fragile and likely to be transitional. (Even the long personalistic regime of Ethiopia has come to an end.) The dominant—in fact, almost universal—political arrangement is a hegemony of the central military force over the paramilitary and national police forces. This observation does not disregard the crucial day-to-day reliance on paramilitary and national police forces. Nor does it avoid examination of the explicit efforts, in nations like India, to develop and expand the paramilitary units in order to relieve the armed forces of tactical involvement in coercive control. However, the strategic and fundamental balance of power and coercion is what is critical. Typically, paramilitary units and the national police force are organized under the ministry of the interior or a comparable ministry. But separate organization does not mean an independent political existence. The paramilitary forces are not only adjuncts of the central military forces, they also have a parallel relation to the political police. The political police are able to perform their day-to-day repressive functions because of the constant presence of the visible and mobile manpower of the paramilitary units.

In the extreme, the armed forces can demonstrate their supremacy over the paramilitary units by outright assault on paramilitary and police units. For example, in Peru in 1975 the military regime used its active-duty personnel to attack frontally strongpoints held by the local police. Routinely and typically, organizational factors—of both weaponry and logistics—guarantee the dominance of the armed forces over the paramilitary and the national police. This dominance is reinforced by the military organizations' claims that they represent the nation as a whole and by their presenting themselves as agencies for achieving national goals. The police and paramilitary are defined in more delimited terms and with a symbolism of coercive control.

A series of institutional arrangements link the military and the paramilitary forces. The military often supply the weapons and training for paramilitary forces and carry out inspections. Frequently personnel are interchanged, especially at the higher levels, and such exchanges are designed to reinforce the dominance of the armed forces. Of course, these formal arrangements are augmented—and sometimes complicated—by informal and systematic techniques of political surveillance, including the penetration of military units by political police. In varying formats, we are dealing with a division of labor among the central military, the paramilitary, and the political police. We think of the division of labor in the economic and industrial sector of society, but the same idea applies to the institutions of coercion. The organization and skills required by the central military forces are incompatible or at least very different from those needed for the paramilitary units. This is especially so in that minority of the developing countries which use conscripts. Likewise, the milieu of the political police tends to differentiate it from the regular professional miiltary units.

However, the structure and extent of coercive control in most of the developing nations cannot be described as totalitarian—they represent a much more primitive apparatus and a milder form of authoritarian regime. By "totalitarian regime" we refer not only to the greater intensity of coercion but also to scope; in a totalitarian regime the scope of repression is, in effect, universal penetration of all sectors and dimensions of the society. The natural history of the coercive agencies of a totalitarian regime—for example, Nazi Germany—and that of a typical developing nation are very different. In Nazi Germany, the Nazi party inherited the complex administrative apparatus of the existing police and military institutions, and it could refashion these to meet its own needs. In addition, the mechanisms of repression evolved from the structure and the agencies of the Nazi party itself—that is, of a mass political movement designed to seize power and to destroy the sources of political opposition. The central agencies of the Nazi security system—the SD (*Sicherheitsdienst*), the SS (*Schutzstaffel*), and the SA (*Sturmabteilung*)—originated as party organs under the complete control of the party cadres.[21] They became "official" agencies of the state after the Nazi seizure of power, and through them the Nazi movement dominated the existing security agencies and in time the military establishment itself.

In contrast, except for those few new nations that engaged in extensive military or paramilitary operations to obtain national independence, the political regime of the "typical" new nation found itself with limited and fragmented security agencies. Such a political regime was the outgrowth of agitational movements

[21] Franz Neumann, *Behemoth: The Structure and Practice of National Socialism* (Toronto and New York: Oxford University Press, 1942).

and hardly rested on elaborate administrative structures. Where there was a prolonged military struggle, the political movements and military formations developed more extensive security and surveillance forces that were then available for coercive control—for example, in Algeria. However, in general the political regime had to build internal security and paramilitary forces from the limited resources that the colonial government left behind. In this area, institution building faced barriers and resistance comparable to those encountered in other sectors of society in the developing nations.

Thus it may be argued that a totalitarian society rests on an administrative and technological base that had not been forged in the nations that have gained independence after 1945. Likewise, in Latin American countries, in general, military regimes until the middle of the 1960s rested on a limited apparatus of police control. Of course, there have been political regimes with very repressive and coercive controls without an urbanized or industrialized base. Nevertheless, the persistent and extensive imprisonment of large numbers of civilians in concentration camps—a crucial indicator of totalitarianism—is an attribute of modern nations or of nations determined to industrialize rapidly.

In other words, the relatively limited coercive control system that characterizes the modal developing nations is a function of an elite perspective on the pace and direction of internal sociopolitical change. One of the main emphases of the elites of new nations has been the gradual but steady expulsion of "undesirable" aliens—not merely ex-colonials but also persons from adjoining nations. The amount of coercive power required is limited, although the results have been extremely painful and cruel to those involved. The expulsion technique has relieved the elites from having to maintain internal concentration camps like those in the Soviet Union and Nazi Germany, whose elites had a comprehensive conception of the need for coercive control.[22]

[22] Barrington Moore, Jr., *Terror and Progress USSR: Some Sources of Change and Stability in the Soviet Dictatorship* (Cambridge: Harvard University Press, 1954).

Some totalitarian controls do emerge when new nations develop schemes of agricultural collectivization and ruthlessly move large numbers of the farming population into new settlements, as has been done experimentally in, for example, Tanzania. Likewise, in some developing nations (for example, Brazil and Chile), military regimes engage on occasion in brutal repression. We have very little reliable information about the extent of networks of informers and political police in the developing nations. However, by the standards of performance in the Soviet Union or Nazi Germany, the degree of repression is indeed limited.

In the light of these observations it is possible to examine the data presented in table 1, which describes the patterns of growth for both the central military forces (including reserve units) and the paramilitary forces. These data are for the decade from 1966 to 1974/75 and are designed to augment the statistical presentation in the earlier edition.[23] The data are worldwide, to encompass Latin America and to make comparisons between industrialized and developing nations possible.

In table 1 the data are organized by the official United Nations regions—which are not necessarily the most revealing for our purposes. Later an alternative grouping in terms of political and cultural areas is presented; but the UN categories supply a point of departure. For the entire continent of Africa, during the period from 1966 to 1975, manpower in the total regular military forces increased from 501,500 to 938,100, or 86 percent. At the same time, the paramilitary forces increased from 224,100 to 427,300, or 91 percent. It should be noted, however, that a significant amount of the growth in military manpower was in two countries—Nigeria and Egypt. Nigeria went through a major civil war; Egypt fought two major engagements with Israel. Internal political pressures in Nigeria have prevented a reduction of military manpower; and the absence of a political resolution of the Middle East conflict has meant that the Egyptian forces have been maintained at wartime levels. If these two nations are removed

23 See below, pp. 86–87.

from the tabulation, the relatively greater growth in the paramilitary forces than in the regular forces is marked. For the remaining nations of Africa, the regular military expanded from 313,500 to 463,100, or 48 percent, compared with 144 percent (134,100 to 327,300) in paramilitary units for comparable African nations.

For the Asia region the figures for the regular military indicate an expansion from 7,397,500 to 9,629,900, or 30 percent. These reflect the intensification of military conflict in Southeast Asia and the war between India and Pakistan. By contrast, the paramilitary forces increased from 3,377,000 to 5,904,100, or 74 percent. Thus, in absolute number as well as percentage, the increase of paramilitary personnel was greater than that of the regular forces in the Asia region.

In South America the same pattern of greater increase in the paramilitary has also emerged, but on a much more limited scale in both absolute and proportionate terms—reflecting the continued low concentrations of military and paramilitary personnel there. The figures for the decade under consideration for the regular military forces revealed an increase from 605,100 to 639,200, or only 6 percent, while for the paramilitary units the growth was much more marked, from 232,300 to 305,300, or 30.5 percent.

For our purposes it is appropriate to group the developing nations into the political and cultural areas of the Middle East, Asia, Sub-Sahara Africa, South America, and Central America. By excluding China we have the following groupings for comparable analysis of both military and paramilitary personnel, and as rubrics for tracing the natural history of sociopolitical movements:

Middle East: Algeria, Egypt, Iran, Iraq, Israel, Jordan, Lebanon, Libya, Morocco, Saudi Arabia, Somalia, Sudan, Syria, Tunisia, Turkey, Yemen (North and South).

Asia: Afghanistan, Bangladesh, Burma, Ceylon, India, Indonesia, Korea (North), Korea (South), Malaysia, Nepal, Pakistan, the Philippines, Singapore, Taiwan, Thailand. (The states of Indochina are excluded.)

TABLE 1

World Profile of Armed Forces, 1966–75
By United Nations Regions

COUNTRY	POPULATION 1974 Est. (MILLIONS)	ACTIVE-DUTY MILITARY 1966	ACTIVE-DUTY MILITARY 1974/75	RESERVES 1974/75	PARAMILITARY 1966*	PARAMILITARY 1974/75
AFRICA						
1. Nigeria	61.0	8,000	157,000	12,000	8,000 (1968)	40,000
2. Egypt	36.6	180,000	298,000	534,000	90,000 (1969)	100,000
3. Ethiopia	26.9	30,000	44,500	...	4,500 (1969)	20,400
4. Zaire	24.7	35,000	50,000	...	10,000 (1970)†	12,000
5. S. Africa	24.6	26,500	47,400	72,000	51,000 (1966)	75,000†
6. Sudan	17.4	12,000	38,600	...	3,000 (1970)	5,000
7. Morocco	16.8	35,000	56,000	...	3,000 (1968)	23,000
8. Algeria	16.4	65,000	63,000	50,000	8,000 (1968)	10,000
9. Tanzania	14.7	1,500	11,600	...	500 (1970)	500
10. Kenya	12.9	3,000	7,400	...	500 (1970)	1,800
11. Uganda	11.1	2,000	12,600	...	5,500 (1967)	15,000
12. Ghana	9.6	9,000	17,700	...	3,000 (1970)	3,000
13. Malagasy	7.4	4,000	4,200	...	4,000 (1970)	4,000
14. Cameroon	6.3	2,800	5,500	...	5,000 (1972)	10,000
15. Rhodesia	6.1	4,500	4,700	10,000	6,400 (1970)	8,000 / 35,000†
16. Upper Volta	5.9	1,000	2,000	...	1,800 (1967)	2,100
17. Tunisia	5.6	20,000	24,000	...	5,000 (1970)	10,000
18. Mali	5.5	3,000	3,600	...	1,500 (1970)	2,700
19. Malawi	4.9	1,500	1,600	...	...	...
20. Ivory Coast	4.7	3,500	3,500	...	1,700 (1970)	3,000
21. Zambia	4.6	2,500	5,800	...	800 (1970)	1,200
22. Niger	4.4	2,000	2,100	...	1,600 (1970)	1,400
23. Guinea	4.3	5,000	5,500	...	7,000 (1970)	8,000
24. Senegal	4.3	5,000	5,900	...	...	1,600
25. Rwanda	4.1	1,000	2,700	...	600 (1970)	700
26. Chad	4.0	400	4,100	...	3,800 (1971)	6,000
27. Burundi	3.5	1,000	2,000	...	800 (1967)	900

36

28.	Somalia	3.1	6,000	17,300	...	500 (1970)	3,500
29.	Dahomey	3.0	1,000	1,500	...	1,000 (1967)	1,000
30.	Sierra Leone	2.7	1,300	1,600	...	...	...
31.	Libya	2.2	5,500	25,000	...	...	23,000
32.	Togo	2.2	1,000	1,200	...	1,000 (1967)	1,000
33.	Liberia	2.0	3,800	5,100	...	700 (1967)	1,300
34.	Central Afr. Republic	1.5	1,200	1,300	...	...	...
35.	Mauritania	1.3	1,000	1,800	...	400 (1967)	1,100
36.	Congo (Brazzaville)	1.0	1,500	2,300	...	1,500 (1971)	4,800
	SUBTOTAL	367.3	501,500	938,100	678,000	224,100	427,300

ASIA

1.	China	800.0	2,614,000	2,900,000	5,000,000	250,000 (1967)	300,000
2.	India	588.5	550,000	956,000	230,000	100,000 (1966)	200,000
3.	Indonesia	126.8	350,000	270,000		20,000 (1966)	120,000
4.	Japan	109.3	223,000	266,000	39,600	...	...
5.	Bangladesh	65.3		26,500			
6.	Pakistan	58.8	260,000	392,000	513,000	3,700 (1967)	29,000
7.	Philippines	41.4	28,500	42,000	218,500	15,500 (1966)	40,000
8.	Turkey	38.9	452,000	453,000	775,000	55,000 (1967)	84,000
9.	Thailand	38.6	134,000	180,000	200,000	33,000 (1966)	75,000
10.	S. Korea	33.7	575,000	625,000	1,125,000	1,000,000 (1966)	63,000
11.	Iran	32.2	150,000	211,500	300,000	25,000 (1966)	2,000,000†
12.	Burma	30.2	149,000	149,000		25,000 (1970)	70,000
13.	N. Viet Nam‡	23.1	250,000	578,000		20,000 (1966)	35,000
							20,000
						200,000†	420,000†
14.	S. Viet Nam‡	20.3	225,000	572,000			15,000
							570,000†
15.	Afghanistan	18.7	90,000	86,500	164,000	13,000 (1971)	21,000
16.	Taiwan	16.0	542,000	491,000	1,050,000	175,000 (1966)†	175,000†
17.	N. Korea	15.5	309,000	467,000	290,000	25,000 (1966)	50,000
						1,250,000†	1,250,000†
18.	Ceylon	13.6	8,800	13,600	13,100	12,800 (1970)	16,300
19.	Nepal	11.9	20,800	20,500			
20.	Malaysia	11.5	7,600	56,000	26,400	23,000 (1966)	54,000

* Or closest year for which data are available.
† Militia.

TABLE 1—Continued

COUNTRY	POPULATION 1974 EST. (MILLIONS)	ACTIVE-DUTY MILITARY 1966	ACTIVE-DUTY MILITARY 1974/75	RESERVES 1974/75	PARAMILITARY 1966*	PARAMILITARY 1974/75
ASIA—Continued						
21. Iraq	10.7	80,000	101,800	268,000	10,000 (1967)	19,800
22. Saudi Arabia	8.7	30,000	43,000	...	20,000 (1967)	32,500
23. Cambodia†	7.4	32,000	187,200	...	60,000 (1967)	150,000
24. N. Yemen	6.3	10,000 (total)	20,900	...	...	...
25. S. Yemen	1.6		9,500	...	...	...
25. Syria	7.1	60,000	137,500	203,500	8,000 (1967)	9,500
26. Israel	3.3	75,000	115,000	185,000	...	9,000
27. Laos†	3.3	94,000	62,800 Royal 35,000 Pathet Lao	...	22,000 (1967) Royal	40,000
28. Lebanon	3.1	10,800	15,200	...	2,500 (1967)	5,000
29. Jordan	2.6	35,000	37,500	20,000	8,500 (1967)	22,000
30. Singapore	2.2	...	21,700	30,000	...	9,000
SUBTOTAL	2150.6	7,397,500	9,629,900	10,651,000	3,377,000	5,904,100
EUROPE						
1. W. Germany	62.1	430,000	490,000	630,000	30,000 (1966)	20,000
2. United Kingdom	56.2	435,000	354,600	429,500	...	...
3. Italy	55.1	390,000	421,000	645,000	85,000 (1966)	80,000
4. France	52.0	880,400	502,500	450,000	75,000 (1966)	85,000
5. Spain	35.2	400,000	284,000		65,000 (1970)	65,000
6. Poland	33.4	285,000	280,000	600,000	45,000 (1966)	73,000 350,000†
7. Rumania	21.2	218,000	171,000	435,000	50,000 (1966)	40,000 500,000†
8. Yugoslavia	21.1	347,000	230,000	...	19,000 (1966)	19,000 1,010,000†
9. E. Germany	17.0	154,000	145,000	260,000	70,000 (1966)	80,000 400,000†
10. Czechoslovakia	14.5	185,000	200,000	350,000	35,000 (1966)	35,000 250,000†

11. Netherlands	13.5	130,000	113,900	338,300	3,000 (1970)	3,700
12. Hungary	10.5	90,000	103,000	163,000	35,000 (1966)	4,000†
13. Belgium	9.8	110,000	89,700	15,600	12,000 (1968)	25,000
14. Portugal	9.2	190,000	217,000	318,000	10,000 (1966)	250,000†
15. Greece	9.0	161,000	161,200	275,000	73,000 (1967)	15,000
16. Bulgaria	8.7	149,500	152,000	285,000	15,000 (1969)	9,700
17. Sweden	8.2	70,200	72,200	750,000	…	99,000
18. Austria	7.5	24,600	42,000	112,700	12,000 (1970)	20,000
19. Switzerland	6.6	31,500	42,500	582,000	…	150,000†
20. Denmark	5.1	42,500	37,100	138,000	…	…
21. Finland	4.7	41,900	35,800	685,000	3,000 (1966)	11,200
22. Norway	4.0	32,000	34,900	174,500	3,000 (1966)	…
23. Ireland	3.1	13,000	12,300	19,800	…	3,700
24. Albania	2.4	28,000	38,000	100,000	12,500 (1966)	…
SUBTOTAL	470.1	4,837,600	4,225,000	7,070,800	652,500	15,000
NORTH AND CENTRAL AMERICA						
1. U.S.A.	213.5	2,702,000	2,174,000	883,000	…	…
2. Mexico	56.4	62,200	71,000	250,000§	…	…
3. Canada	22.6	119,700	83,000	17,700	13,000 (1970)	13,000
4. Cuba	9.1	43,000	116,500	200,000†	3,000 (1970)	3,000
5. Guatemala	5.6	8,000	11,200	…	12,500 (1967)	14,900
6. Haiti	5.3	5,000	6,500	…	10,000 (1967)	10,000
7. Dominican Republic	4.5	19,000	15,800	…	2,500 (1967)	3,000
8. El Salvador	3.9	4,000	5,100	…	2,500 (1967)	2,600
9. Honduras	2.9	2,500	5,700	…	4,000 (1970)	4,000
10. Nicaragua	2.2	5,000	7,100	…	…	1,200
11. Costa Rica	1.8	…	…	…	…	6,000
12. Panama	1.5	…	…	…	3,700 (1967)	…
SUBTOTAL	329.3	2,970,400	2,495,900	1,350,700	51,200	57,700

† As of 1974.
§ Part-time conscripts.

TABLE 1—*Continued*

Country	Population 1974 Est. (Millions)	Active-Duty Military 1966	Active-Duty Military 1974/75	Reserves 1974/75	Paramilitary 1966*	Paramilitary 1974/75
OCEANIA						
1. Australia............	13.0	52,000	68,800	27,700	...	...
2. New Zealand........	3.0	12,500	12,600	7,400	...	...
Subtotal............	16.00	64,500	81,400	35,100	...	...
U.S.S.R.						
U.S.S.R.............	252.5	3,850,000	3,525,000	3,000,000	230,000 (1967)	300,000
SOUTH AMERICA						
1. Brazil.............	104.7	272,700	208,000		120,000 (1967)	150,000
2. Argentina.........	24.6	116,000	135,000	250,000	10,000 (1967)	19,000
3. Colombia..........	23.7	60,000	63,200	250,000	30,000 (1967)	35,000
4. Peru..............	15.4	37,000	54,000	...	18,500 (1970)	20,000
5. Venezuela.........	11.7	19,700	39,000	...	8,000 (1967)	10,000
6. Chile.............	10.4	42,300	60,000	160,000	22,000 (1967)	30,000
7. Ecuador..........	6.9	15,800	22,300	...	5,800 (1967)	5,800
8. Bolivia...........	5.4	15,000	21,800	...	3,000 (1967)	5,000
9. Uruguay..........	3.0	17,000	21,000	100,000	10,000 (1967)	22,000
10. Paraguay.........	2.8	9,600	14,900	...	5,000 (1967)	8,500
Subtotal............	208.6	605,100	639,200	760,000	232,300	305,300

40

Sub-Sahara Africa: Burundi, Cameroon, Central African Republic, Chad, Congo (Brazzaville), Dahomey, Ethiopia, Ghana, Guinea, Ivory Coast, Kenya, Liberia, Malagasy, Malawi, Mali, Mauritania, Niger, Nigeria, Rwanda, Senegal, Sierra Leone, Tanzania, Togo, Uganda, Upper Volta, Zaire, Zambia.
South America: Argentina, Bolivia, Brazil, Chile, Colombia, Ecuador, Paraguay, Peru, Uruguay, Venezuela.
Central America: Costa Rica, Cuba, Dominican Republic, El Salvador, Guatemala, Haiti, Honduras, Mexico, Nicaragua, Panama.

In table 2 our tabulations are presented; they confirm the trend of increase for the paramilitary forces of the developing nations. In Asia and South America the paramilitary personnel have increased at a higher rate than regular active-duty military personnel. In each of the other areas the overall figures are distorted by growth in a single country that has been engaged in active hostilities. If we remove Nigeria, Cuba, and Egypt, we highlight the growth of the paramilitary in Sub-Sahara Africa, Central America, and to a lesser extent the Middle East.

The growth of paramilitary personnel is a worldwide trend. It occurs in the industrialized nations, but at varying rates. In the nations of Western Europe during the decade, there has been a 15.5 percent reduction of active-duty military personnel and a growth in the paramilitary personnel from 346,000 to 377,000, or 9.0 percent. In Eastern Europe, while active-duty personnel have risen from 1,285,000 to 1,317,000, or 2.5 percent, paramilitary personnel have increased by 9.2 percent (from 272,000 to 295,000). However, in the U.S.S.R. the number of paramilitary personnel has increased much more—from 230,000 to 300,000, or 30.4 percent—while active-duty military personnel have declined. In the United States, the National Guard is the closest equivalent to paramilitary forces, although it has a dual mission, since it is an integral element in the national defense force. However, since 1966 the National Guard has declined from approximately 420,000 to 410,000, or 2.3 percent.

TABLE 2

WORLD PROFILE OF ARMED FORCES, 1966–75*

BY POLITICAL AND CULTURAL AREAS

(DATA PRESENTED IN THOUSANDS)

	1966		1974/75		PERCENT CHANGE	
	ACTIVE DUTY	PARA-MILITARY	ACTIVE DUTY	PARA-MILITARY	ACTIVE DUTY	PARA-MILITARY
Middle East........	1,327	238	1,804	316	+35.9 +28.2†	+32.7
Asia...............	3,025	284	4,036	721	+33.4	+153.9
Sub-Sahara Africa...	132	57	364	104	+175.0 +67.8‡	+82.5
South America......	605	232	639	305	+5.6	+30.5
Central America.....	149	51	239	58	+40.0 +4.2§	+13.7
Western Europe......	3,200	346	2,705	377	−15.5	+9.0
East Europe........	1,285	272	1,317	295	+2.5	+9.2
U.S.S.R............	3,850	230	3,525	300	−8.5	+30.4

* This tabulation excludes militia forces.
† Without Egypt.
‡ Without Nigeria.
§ Without Cuba.

During 1965–75, the decade under analysis, there have been notable increases in population. I have therefore calculated, but not reported in this essay, the ratios of military personnel to total population, and of paramilitary personnel to total population, for each nation. This standardization produces the same results and at certain points even stronger documentation of the underlying trend.

Finally, classifying the developing nations by size is useful not only for charting trends in military personnel but also for analyzing military coups and regime consolidation. In fact, size is an important characteristic of nation-states in general and of the developing nations in particular. We have eliminated from consideration all developing nations with a population base of less than one million in 1966; even then, the typical developing nation is small in population and area. Most of the population of the developing nations reside in a limited number of nation-states that are very large. After we have eliminated those nations with less than one million and have focused on the states of Central America, South America, Africa, and Asia (excluding China), we have a total of seventy-eight nation-states. In this group, India, Indonesia, and Brazil have populations of over 100 million each. In 1974 India had 588.5 million; Indonesia, 126.8 million; and Brazil, 104.7 million (see table 3). These three nations contain 47.8 percent of the population of our universe of developing countries. If we extend our list to include those nations with over 25 million each in population, we have fifteen. (The additional countries, arranged by size, are Bangladesh, Nigeria, Pakistan, Mexico, the Philippines, Turkey, Thailand, Egypt, South Korea, Iran, Burma, and Ethiopia.) These fifteen nations contain 78.1 percent of the population of the developing countries. By examining these nations case by case, we can obtain an overview of the sociopolitical transformation of the new nations and of those of Latin America. These fifteen nations also have the majority of the paramilitary forces of the developing nations.

TABLE 3

POPULATION CONCENTRATION OF
15 LARGEST DEVELOPING NATIONS, 1974
(PRESENTED IN PERCENTAGE AND CUMULATIVE PERCENTAGE
OF NEW DEVELOPING NATIONS POPULATION)

	POPULATION 1974 (MILLIONS)	PERCENTAGE	CUMULATIVE PERCENTAGE
India	588.5	34.3	34.3
Indonesia	126.8	7.4	41.7
Brazil	104.7	6.1	47.8
Bangladesh	65.5	3.8	51.6
Nigeria	61.0	3.6	55.2
Pakistan	58.8	3.4	58.6
Mexico	56.4	3.3	61.9
Philippines	41.4	2.4	64.3
Turkey	38.9	2.3	66.6
Thailand	38.6	2.2	68.8
Egypt	36.6	2.1	70.9
South Korea	33.7	2.0	72.9
Iran	32.2	1.9	74.8
Burma	30.2	1.8	76.6
Ethiopia	26.9	1.6	78.2
SUBTOTAL 15 LARGEST DEVELOPING NATIONS	1,340.2	78.2	
TOTAL DEVELOPING NATIONS OVER ONE MILLION	1,716.5	100.0	

CONSEQUENCES FOR REGIME CONSOLIDATION

Is it possible to offer any observations about the consequences of the growth of paramilitary forces for the stability and consolidation of political regimes in the developing nations—in the new nations of Africa, the Middle East, and Asia, as well as in South and Central America? The expansion of the paramilitary forces of the developing nations is a reaction to day-to-day events more than it is an expression of a grand design. One important source of pressure for enlarging internal police agencies is the specter and the reality of university students in revolt. A regime rapidly becomes preoccupied with controlling the outbursts of students, especially those in residence at the national university located in the capital city. From Bangkok to Mexico City, the record shows very sharp interventions.

Paramilitary forces are defined as instruments for controlling unrest and mob action in the urban population at large as well. These paramilitary forces are deployed in the continuous task of policing the potentially disruptive groupings of resistance or opposition to the central regime—regional, religious, or ethnic minorities who feel excluded from the existing political arrangements.

The definition of internal policing emphasizes intervention in rural areas, including the most remote regions, loci of discontent, conventional banditry, and various forms of parapolitical and political agitation. A military regime presses and succeeds in introducing land reform, often after civilian regimes have been unable to do so. The central government assumes that, to implement this objective, it must have effective paramilitary forces at its disposal to symbolize its authority and to overcome, by a show of strength, resistance to its land reform programs and, in turn, to maintain an element of stability in the accompanying period of turmoil. Only as a last resort, when paramilitary units are unable to cope with uprisings and disorder, do the regular military forces become directly involved in rural policing.

In the most fundamental sense, paramilitary units serve as political elements in the continuous internal bargaining. The role of paramilitary agencies in the internal security operations of a developing nation articulates with the political tactics of the regular military's leaders. As the regular military become involved in domestic politics, they initially operate through personal and conspiratorial networks and employ secrecy and selective coercive controls. But eventually they become involved in particular civilian linkages and thereby find themselves enlarging their networks into loose factions. In this process they must rely more and more on bargaining and negotiations. It is not an error to speak of the civilianization of military regimes. Under these conditions, the military must rely heavily on paramilitary units to control sectors of the civilian population, especially those—religious, ethnic, or linguistic—that are not incorporated in this submerged and half-hidden political bargaining.

In general, paramilitary forces expand under military regimes—whether they be military oligarchies or regimes dominated by a single leader. The modal pattern in the new nations is that of an interventionist regime that comes to operate with some form of rhetoric about economic and social change grounded in governmentalized or socialistic enterprise. Since the early 1960s, this trend has emerged in Latin America. Our case-by-case examination has demonstrated that paramilitary and national police systems can also expand rapidly under civilian regimes, as in India and the Philippines, and can thereby supply the basis for authoritarian trends under civilian leadership. Moreover, an interventionist posture does not rest exclusively on a left-wing orientation, although it is more likely to be leftist. Iran is but one example of a rightist regime that has adopted intervention policies of land reform and centrally stimulated economic growth. The military coup in Bangladesh in 1975 had strong Islamic and conservative overtones.

Time perspective is an important dimension of an interventionist outlook. An interventionist policy means that the military elite—even reluctantly and under pressure—must think in longer than immediate terms. In the conventional military coup in Latin America, supplying a new political balance for the moment has been the essential goal. But interventionist policies require some perspective on the future—at least a debate about how long a period will be required, or even if a "permanent" regime will be required, to effect the desired transformation. In making these calculations—however vague and disjointed—the military regime comes to appreciate the increased importance of the paramilitary agencies in the immediate day-to-day management of the nation-state. Again and again, one notes the conscious effort made by military officials to remove their regular units from the distasteful tasks of internal security. They believe this removal is necessary if the political legitimacy and the effectiveness of their regime are to be enhanced and the internal cohesion of their military formations is to be maintained. Of course, with the passage of time, vested interests operate to perpetuate military regimes, and the rewards of corruption are among the most powerful pressures.

One can offer a simplistic economic and evolutionary overview of the role of the military in sociopolitical change and in achieving stability in the developing nations, and such a formulation has relevance, if only as a debater's point. Before World War II, military intervention in Latin America, with the exception of Mexico, can be considered as an early stage of politico-military involvement.[24] In this view, the military espoused the interests of the privileged groups in the society, including the gradually expanding middle class. There is some support for such an orientation, although the middle class may well have been better off with a more capitalistic political economy. However, the Russian and Chinese revolutions altered the setting of the post–World War II ex-colonial world. The sociopolitical tasks and goals require addressing the aspirations of submerged groups—peasants and urban workers. To rule, the military have had, for regime stability and consolidation, to develop mechanisms for incorporating these social groups, even if these mechanisms have involved symbolic manipulation and a strong component of coercive control.

Of course, one is tempted to separate the "economic" factor from the "coercive" factor by statistical analysis, despite analytical and empirical difficulties. It is necessary to recall our earlier observation that military regimes per se are no more and no less likely than civilian regimes to generate economic development as measured, for example, by rate of growth. Even if they were, it would be extremely difficult to assess the distribution of the results of economic development. In other words, there is no need to assume that a military regime inherently has either advantages

[24] Edwin Liewen, *Mexican Militarism: The Political Rise and Fall of the Revolutionary Army* (Albuquerque: University of New Mexico Press, 1957), p. 44.

or disadvantages in consolidating power because of its economic performance. If certain ones do, it is because they exploit their natural resources, although there are isolated cases of the growth of an effective industrial base, as for example in Brazil. It also appears that foreign military assistance programs are not decisive or even influential in accounting for a military regime's ability or inability to consolidate its rule.

Obviously none of these specific observations is offered to negate the general importance of managing economic resources for regime consolidation. Recruiting and maintaining an effective paramilitary force require economic resources. Paramilitary forces are inexpensive compared to regular forces, since there is little investment in elaborate military equipment. However, when their costs are added to those for the regular armed forces, the totals are heavy for a developing nation. The careful tabulations of military expenditures prepared by the United States Arms Control and Disarmament Agency indicate that the rate of growth for military expenditures and armed forces in the developing nations is higher than the rate in the developed nations.[25] By 1972 the share of the developing countries' GNP devoted to military expenditures was approaching that of developed countries. The lower per capita incomes of the developing nations, however, make their military expenditures much more burdensome than those of the industrialized nations.

Although there have been military mutinies because of dissatisfaction with wages, in general the developing nations have been able to satisfy such demands fairly effectively. (Such mutinies occurred in Kenya, Uganda, and Tanganyika in 1964 and required the intervention of British soldiers.) Developing nations may not be able to enlarge their armed forces as much as their elites desire, but the standard of living of their military and paramilitary personnel is relatively privileged. Among civilian elites and the popu-

25 U.S. Arms Control and Disarmament Agency, *World Military Expenditures and Arms Trade, 1963–1973* (Washington, D.C.: Government Printing Office, 1974), pp. 1–3.

lace at large, however, the prestige of such personnel is usually not very high.

It is possible that long-term economic stagnation or even particular economic disasters, such as widespread famine, crop failure, or massive economic mismanagement, could undermine a regime's ability to equip and pay its military personnel. The loyalty of such personnel would be undermined and their continued viability theatened. Katherine Chorley has written about this subject, drawing on the historical experiences of Western Europe.[26] The prospect of military disintegration under economic hardship conjures up alarming images, since the collapse of military units only produces new and unanticipated forms of coercion. If there is no external intervention, there may well be prolonged political violence—even civil war—between remnants of the central military and informal paramilitary groups and irregular formations. The trend, in such an event, could be toward forms of more authoritarian political control in which the successful political groups would rely on politicalized paramilitary formations.

It must be emphasized, however, that with rare exceptions military coups and military interventions in the developing nations since 1945 have not been generated because economic stress has weakened or disintegrated the military and its associated units. These military interventions have rather been the deliberate response of organized factions whose leaders have sought to increase their power or have felt that the existing regime—civilian or military—had failed to achieve goals of economic and social improvement.

The prevailing image of the developing nations is one of persistent and at moments almost random instability. Reporting on the politics of these nations, even in the informed mass media, stresses sudden shifts in regimes. In reality, however, there are both a crude pattern in these shifts and more stability or at least more continuity than is usually supposed. Indications of trends

[26] Katherine Chorley, *Armies and the Art of Revolution* (London: Faber and Faber, 1943).

toward regime consolidation can be observed, if only because the goals the elites set for themselves have been moderated. (A few nations, it is true, display the pattern of chronic instability.) The tempo of movement toward regime persistence varies from one political and cultural area to another, and in each region there are nation-states that deviate from the pattern. But the overall trend toward regime consolidation since 1965 has been so marked that we would have to speak of a redirection or a new phase if instability were to increase.

At this point we can proceed on the basis of a crude, simple, yet very revealing indicator: military coups from 1945 to 1975. One could have anticipated a random distribution or a sheer persistence in the level of coups. Instead we would anticipate finding, within each region, a pattern of declining frequency of successful coups. More precisely, we would expect the decline to occur in three phases. In the first, there would be few if any coups. In the next, coups would become more frequent. Finally, the number of coups would decline, reflecting the search for a new balance, even though that balance might be partial, short-lived, or unstable. The onset of the latter phase would vary from region to region and in part would reflect the patterns of diffusion in the particular area. The whole process might also continue into the future, beyond the period of our analysis.

It should be recalled that this pattern of regime consolidation is grounded in the natural history perspective toward sociopolitical movements. It is a delimited tool of analysis and not a global theory of history. In this view, the trend is from limited objectives to more comprehensive goals of sociopolitical change to, finally, the emergence of more limited and diverse goals. We are essentially interested in the ability of an elite to maintain itself in power. Regime stability does not rely solely on the ability of a particular leader or of a particular junta to retain power. It also involves the crucial question of leadership succession. With the passage of time, more and more developing nations have had to face this issue.

Egypt, both in its natural history and in its leadership succession, is a polar example that conforms to our model. (Argentina, as described below, may well be taken as the polar example that does not conform.) Egypt's limited and moderate effort to achieve change had its origins in the period after 1945. However, the first phase of its natural history was signaled by Nagub's coup in 1952, with its nationalist aspiration and its objectives for limited sociopolitical change. The second and more interventionist period, both externally and internally, came with the Nasser coup in 1954. The Nasser regime was a period of activist and extremist intervention in the domestic economy and in a militant pan-Arab foreign policy. The failure of its attempts led to gradual "retreat." The Nasser regime developed enough internal consolidation so that Sadat could become president in 1971 and prime minister in 1973 in an orderly process of succession. One can mark the shift to the subsequent phase in 1973, after the Yom Kippur war, when the trend toward a moderated political and economic policy has become dominant and a more flexible foreign policy has emerged.

To what extent has the experience of Egypt—and the natural history of its internal, sociopolitical movements—been typical or at least repeated among the developing nations? In exploring regional patterns, we must take into consideration the concentration of frequent coups—successful ones, at that—in a few nation-states.

We have documented, in our sample of seventy-eight nation-states, 128 successful coups for the three decades since the end of World War II, that is, from 1945 to 1975. (See table 4.) In statistical terms, this would mean slightly more than 1.5 coups per nation-state. However, the frequency is not equally distributed. There are twenty-two developing nations that did not experience a successful military coup between 1945 and 1975. (Since 1975 successful coups have occurred in some of these nations.) On the other hand, four countries, in different regions, account for 28 of the successful military coups, or 21 percent of the total number. (The coup-prone nations are Syria, 11; Bolivia, 7; Dahomey, 6; and Haiti, 5. These nations tend to be small; examining the largest

TABLE 4

FREQUENCY OF SUCCESSFUL MILITARY COUPS IN THE DEVELOPING
NATIONS IN THE POST–WORLD WAR II PERIOD
(TABULATED BY FIVE-YEAR PERIODS)

	MIDDLE EAST	ASIA	SUB-SAHARA AFRICA	SOUTH AMERICA	CENTRAL AMERICA
1945–49	3	1	0	8	5
1950–54	5	0	0	6	4
1955–59	2	2	0	5	6
1960–64	8	3	3	6	6
1965–69	8	1	18	5	1
1970–74	1	2	9	5	0
1975–	0	1	2	1	1
TOTAL NO. OF COUPS	27	10	32	36	23
GRAND TOTAL					128
NUMBER OF NATIONS	17	15	26	10	10
GRAND TOTAL					78
TOTAL POPULATION 1972 (MILLIONS)	212.6	1,072.9	238.2	208.6	93.2

fifteen, we find greater stability.) By region, Central and South
America have had the highest frequency of successful military
coups. The rank order of the other regions, roughly speaking,
would be Sub-Sahara Africa, the Middle East, and Asia, if one
takes into account the number of nations and the population base.
(The successful coups during 1945–75 are set forth in table 5.)[27]

The date of independence is only a partial index to the onset
of post-colonial societal transformation. We are dealing with a

27 In addition to the standard newspaper and documentary sources, the
following works were helpful in the preparation of this compilation of successful coups: Claude E. Welch, Jr., "Personalism and Corporatism in African Armies," in Catherine McCardle Kelleher, ed., *Political-Military Systems:
Comparative Perspectives* (Beverly Hills, Calif: Sage Publications, 1974),
pp. 125–46; Eliezer Be'eri, *Army Officers in Arab Politics and Society* (London: Pall Mall, 1970); Mauricio Solaun and Michael A. Quinn, *Sinners and
Heretics: The Politics of Military Intervention in Latin America* (Urbana:
University of Illinois Press, 1973); William R. Thompson, *The Grievances
of Military Coup-Makers*, Sage Professional Papers in Comparative Politics,
no. 01-407 (Beverly Hills, Calif.: Sage Publications, 1973); William G.
Andrews and Uri Ra'anan, eds., *The Politics of the Coup d'Etat: Five Case
Studies* (New York: Van Nostrand Reinhold, 1969).

TABLE 5

Country	Date of Independence	Coup Date	Leader
MIDDLE EAST			
Algeria..........1962		June 1965	Boumediene
Egypt...........Pre–World War II		July 1952	Free Officers
		March 1954	Nasser
Iran............Pre–World War II		August 1953	Zahed
Iraq............1932		July 1958	Qasim
		February 1963	Arif
		November 1963	Arif
		July 1968	al-Bair
Israel...........1948		None	
Jordan...........		None	
Libya...........1951		September 1969	Qaddaffi
Morocco........1956		None	
Saudi Arabia......		None	
Somalia.........1960		October 1969	
Sudan...........1956		November 1958	Abboud
		May 1969	Nimeiri
Syria...........1943		March 1949	Zaim
		August 1949	Hinawr
		December 1949	Shishakir
		November 1951	Shishakir
		February 1954	Abu Assaf
		September 1961	Kuzbari, Nahlawi
		March 1962	Nahlawi
		March 1962	Badr Asan
		March 1963	Hariri
		February 1966	Jadid, Hatum
		February 1969	Hafiz al-Asad
Tunisia..........1956		None	
Turkey..........1919		1922 (not included)	Ataturk
		May 1960	Menduhtagmavc
		March 1971	
Yemen		September 1962	Sallal
		November 1967	al-Iryani
			al-Ayni
ASIA			
Afghanistan......Pre–World War II		July 1973	
Bangladesh.......1971		August 1975	Khondakar Moshtaque Ahmed
Burma..........1948		September 1958	General NeWin
		March 1962	General NeWin
Ceylon..........1947		None	
India...........1947		None	
		State of emergency, 1975	
Indonesia........1948		March 1966	General Suharto
Korea			
South..........1948		April 1960	General Park
		May 1961	
North..........1945			

53

TABLE 5—*Continued*

COUNTRY	DATE OF INDEPENDENCE	COUP DATE	LEADER
		ASIA—*Continued*	
Malaysia.........		None	
Nepal............		None	
Pakistan.........1947		October 1958	General Khan
Philippines.......1946		None	
		Martial Law, September 1972	
Singapore........1965		None	
Taiwan..........1949		None	
Thailand.........Pre–World War II		November 1947	Marshal Lyany P. Saonggram
		November 1971	Field Marshal Thanon Kittikikachorn
		SUB-SAHARA AFRICA	
Burundi..........1962		November 1966	Major Micombero
Cameroon........1960		None	
Central African Republic.......1960		January 1966	Colonel Bokassa
Chad............1960		April 1975	
Congo-Brazzaville.1960		November 1968	Captain Ngouabi
Dahomey.........1960		October 1963	Colonel Soglo
		November 1965	
		December 1965	Colonel Soglo
		December 1966	Major Kouandete
		December 1969	Lt. Colonel Kouandete
		October 1972	Major Kerekou
Ethiopia.........Pre–World War II		October 1974	
Ghana...........1957		February 1966	Colonel Kotoka
			Colonel Ocran
		January 1972	Major Afrififa
			Colonel Acheampong
Guinea...........1958		None	
Ivory Coast......1960		None	
Kenya...........1963		None	
Liberia...........Pre–World War II		None	
Malagasy.....·....1960		May 1973	General Ramamantsoa
		January 1975	
Malawi..........1964		None	
Mali.............1960		November 1968	Captain Djakhite
			Lt. Traore
Mauritania.......1960		None	
Niger............1960		April 1974	
Nigeria..........1960		January 1966	Major Nzeogwu
			Major Ifeajuna
		January 1966	General Ironsi
		July 1966	
		July 1975	Brig. Mohammed
Rwanda..........1962		July 1973	Major General Habyalimana
Senegal..........1960		None	
Sierra Leone......1961		March 1967	Brig. Lansana
		March 1967	Major Blake
		April 1968	

TABLE 5—*Continued*

COUNTRY	DATE OF INDEPENDENCE	COUP DATE	LEADER
SUB-SAHARA AFRICA—*Continued*			
Tanzania	1961	None	
Togo	1960	January 1963	Ex-Sergeant Eyadema
		January 1967	Lt. Colonel Eyadema
Uganda	1962	January 1971	Major General Amin (rank)
Upper Volta	1960	January 1966	Lt. Colonel Lamizana
		February 1974	General Lamizana
Zaire	1960	September 1960	Colonel Mobutu
		November 1965	Major General Mobutu
Zambia	1964	None (Suspension of party rule, April 1975)	
SOUTH AMERICA			
Argentina	Pre–World War II	September 1955	
		November 1955	
		March 1962	
		June 1966	
		June 1970	
Bolivia	Pre–World War II	July 1946	
		May 1951	
		April 1952	
		November 1964	
		September 1969	
		October 1970	
		August 1971	
Brazil	Pre–World War II	August 1954	
		November 1955	
		March 1964	
		August 1969	
Chile	Pre–World War II	September 1973	
Colombia	Pre–World War II	June 1953	
		May 1957	
Ecuador	Pre–World War II	August 1947	
		September 1947	
		July 1963	
		March 1966	
Paraguay	Pre–World War II	June 1948	
		January 1949	
		September 1949	
		May 1954	
		August 1975	
Peru	Pre–World War II	October 1948	
		June 1962	
		March 1963	
		October 1968	
Uruguay	Pre–World War II	1973	
Venezuela	Pre–World War II	November 1948	
		December 1952	
		January 1958	

TABLE 5—*Continued*

COUNTRY	DATE OF INDEPENDENCE	COUP DATE	LEADER
CENTRAL AMERICA			
Costa Rica.......	Pre–World War II	None	
Cuba............	Pre–World War II	March 1952	
Dominican Republic.......	Pre–World War II	June 1962	
		September 1963	
		April 1965	
El Salvador.......	Pre–World War II	December 1948	
		June 1949	
		October 1960	
		June 1961	
Guatemala.......	Pre–World War II	June 1954	
		October 1957	
		March 1963	
Haiti...........	Pre–World War II	January 1946	
		May 1950	
		December 1956	
		February 1957	
		April 1957	
Honduras........	Pre–World War II	October 1956	
		October 1963	
		April 1975	
Mexico..........	Pre–World War II	None	
Nicaragua.......	Pre–World War II	May 1947	
Panama..........	Pre–World War II	November 1949	
		May 1951	

worldwide phenomenon, that is, with the changing relations of the ex-colonial world to the European centers and to the emerging centers of the United States and the Soviet Union. Both close proximity to Europe and the impact of World War II combined to make the Middle East the first region to embark on the politics of domestic intervention. An important part of World War II was fought in the Middle East, and formal independence came there early. In fact, one may assert that the process of decolonization had already started in the Middle East during the aftermath of World War I. But by 1950 these politico-military movements were well under way. On the other hand, Sub-Sahara Africa was less altered by World War II and was more remote from the European center; and decolonization occurred there later. It was not until the second half of the 1960s that interventionist military politics became fully manifest there.

The Asia region is between these two areas in tempo and is closer to the Middle East than to Sub-Sahara Africa. Of course, we are dealing with a much less clearly delimited region, and more with differing subregions, so that the process of diffusion is far less operative. World War II contributed intensely to strengthening nationalist sentiments in Asia, as elsewhere. Asian decolonization started at the war's end but proceeded slowly, with pronounced interruptions. The influences of the competing centers of the Soviet Union and China were felt in varying degrees.[28]

South America and Central America were the last to become involved in these intensified efforts at directed transformation (Mexico's military interventionism was one-half century earlier, but it had no direct consequences for Latin America generally). The Latin American nation-states achieved their formal independence during the nineteenth century; scholars have sought to analyze the particular internal social structure that limited social and economic change. From our point of view, World War II left the region relatively untouched, except for Brazil. The emerging pattern of relations with the United States did not produce directed societal transformation. Military interventionism came last to this region and was accepted with reluctance by military leaders. This phase is represented by a new type of activist coup like that which occurred in Brazil in March 1964, and which departed from the balancing formula of conventional military interventions.

Although we must proceed case by case if we are to describe the natural history pattern, a simple tabulation of the frequency and pattern of successful military coups is revealing. (See table 4.) The earliest outset and diffusion of expanded military interventionism occurred in the Middle East. In the first years after World War II and at the advent of independence, military coups were limited. Their number increased after 1950. After 1970 their de-

[28] Uri Ra'anan, *The USSR Arms the Third World: Case Studies in Soviet Foreign Policy* (Cambridge: MIT Press, 1969).

cline reflects a degree of regime consolidation based on moderated aspirations, increased economic resources, and more effective bureaucratic agencies, including the specially expanded paramilitary forces. In Latin America, on the other hand, the frequency of successful military coups following World War II has been relatively constant, since for most of that period we have been dealing with the "old-fashioned pattern of military coups." After 1965, however, interventionist coups began to emerge in this region, and we can anticipate an increase in regime stability.

Asia presents a very limited number of successful coups with no discernible pattern of diffusion but particular instances of regime consolidation. The Sub-Sahara region shows a sharp rise in 1965–69 and a subsequent decline in the frequency of successful military coups. A case-by-case analysis indicates, however, that as of the middle of the 1970s the process of transformation in the Sub-Sahara is still in its initial stages. Each nation must be examined both individually and in its regional group. Moreover, it must be recalled that the coup-prone nations tend to be small, and that, paradoxically, the large nation-states have developed greater stability.

REGIONAL PATTERNS

When we proceed on a case-by-case analysis, we note that of the seventeen nation-states in the Middle East, six have not had a single successful military coup. In three—Jordan, Morocco, and Saudi Arabia—personal authoritarian regimes have persisted, and it is likely that they will experience military interventionist politics in time.[29] The issue of succession in Tunisia may produce the same pattern; the internal disintegration of Lebanon is a special instance of paramilitary politics.

For the Middle East, Turkey and the regime of Mustafa Kemal Ataturk can be taken as the historical prototype of the military

[29] For the mechanism of personal control of the Jordanian military, see P. J. Vatikiotis, *Politics and the Military in Jordan: A Study of the Arab Legion* (London: Frank Cass, 1967).

regime with interventionist goals that conforms to the natural history model. In 1919–22, during the military struggle for independence, Ataturk represented the first phase of limited reform—that is, strong emphasis on nationalism redefined from the Ottoman Empire and a concern with limited internal change. In this period, he and his cohorts supported the sultan. One of the goals of the National War of Independence was "saving the Sultan and religion." The second activist phase began with the direct assumption of power in 1922 and lasted until 1946. In 1946 the Democratic party was established as an opposition party; in 1950 it came into power, and the role of the military became more circumscribed. The period from 1946 onward can be taken as the third phase, that of movement toward a new balance. It has included a short-term military intervention in 1960 and an even shorter one in 1971, but political emphasis has been on a competitive electoral system.[30] However, the imagery of Turkey is linked to the pre–World War II period.

For the post-World War II period, Egypt not only emerged as the initial example of military interventionist politics but also served as the dominant image during its aspiration for Middle Eastern leadership, when there was an active diffusion of "Nasserism."[31] Syria and Iraq reacted to this influence, and after prolonged political instability reflecting extremist internal policies and external intervention and alliances, both countries have moved toward more stable regimes with more limited sociopolitical objectives. The diffusion process has been at work in the Sudan, Somalia, and Yemen. In the Sudan, the natural history of activist military interventionism was interrupted by civilian rule from 1958 to 1969; but the return of a military regime in 1969 produced

[30] Frederick W. Frey, *The Turkish Elite* (Cambridge: MIT Press, 1965); Ergun Ozbudun, "The Role of the Military in Recent Turkish Politics," Harvard University, Center for International Affairs, Occasional Papers in International Affairs, no. 14, November 1966.
[31] Hrair Dekmejian, *Egypt under Nasir: A Study in Political Dynamics* (Albany: State University of New York Press, 1971); P. J. Vatikiotis, *The Egyptian Army in Politics* (Bloomington: Indiana University Press, 1961).

a leader who has moderated the civil war and sought a new equilibrium.[32] In both Somalia and Yemen, particular features of activist military intervention have remained operative as of 1975. Algeria is the clearest example of the natural history of a revolution. The failure of moderate demands gave way to the emergence of Ben Bella and a period of radical activism, which in turn led to the successful coup by Boumediene in June 1965, which by Algerian standards has represented the movement toward moderation and regime consolidation.[33]

In August 1953 a United States-inspired coup deposed the leftist-oriented prime minister of Iran and created the conditions for Shah Pahlevi's expansion of power. In 1960–61, after announcing projected elections (that did not take place), the shah launched a centralized program of extensive social and economic change including land reform. Iran has experienced rapid economic growth, but the political consolidation of the Pahlevi regime has rested on the enlargement of the internal national security and intelligence service, Savak. This relatively efficient and ruthless agency is concerned with internal opposition—persons and movements. Together with enlarged paramilitary formations, it supplies the shah with the required instruments for internal control. As a personalistic regime, however, Iran is subject to the threat of a factional military coup.

Thus, partially summarizing the Middle East, we can speak of a group of regimes in which the process of military interventionism has not yet started—because of the persistence of authoritarian-personal control (Jordan, Saudi Arabia, Morocco), or because of a charismatic independence leader (Tunisia). For six of the nations (Algeria, Egypt, Iraq, Sudan, Syria, and Turkey), to varying degrees, the notion of a natural history of transformation makes considerable sense. It remains to be seen whether it does for Somalia and Yemen.

[32] Nebor Kasfir, "Civilian Participation under Military Rule in Uganda and Sudan," *Armed Forces and Society* 1 (Spring 1975): 344–63.

[33] William B. Quandt, *Revolution and Political Leadership: Algeria, 1954–1968* (Cambridge: MIT Press, 1969).

Of the fifteen nation-states in the variegated Asia region, seven had not, by 1975, experienced a successful military coup. In fact, the total number of successful coups was only nine in the entire post–World War II period. It is therefore difficult to speak of a diffusion and frequency pattern for these coups, although they were most numerous in 1960–64. (See table 4.) It is striking, however, that the importance of paramilitary forces in this region is not limited to military intervention; such agencies are essential parts of civilian regimes here.

Most of the nations of Asia where there have been no successful military coups represent special cases, often of an authoritarian type. Taiwan is a transposed or rump personal rightist regime that rests on effective political police and paramilitary forces; it has, since 1965, progressively operated with a low profile and quite discreetly. North Korea is the prototype of a Communist regime in which the civilian party dominates the military.[34] The party operates through a paramilitary system that came into being with the withdrawal of the defeated Japanese forces and has remained effective and stable since, in part because of support from the Soviet Union and Red China. As a totalitarian society with a single mass party, North Korea is less likely to experience direct military interventionism—although its military personnel are an important factor in the internal balance and especially in the mechanics of leadership succession. In Thailand a long-standing military regime has repeatedly but temporarily removed itself from political control under the impact of domestic dissatisfaction, but the civilian regime that was constituted in October 1973 has come under enormous opposition pressure and in effect has failed to consolidate its political position.[35]

By 1975 the existing regimes in Ceylon, India, Malaysia, Singapore, and the Philippines, with varying and declining degrees of

[34] Robert A. Scalapino and Chong-sik Lee, *Communism in Korea* (Berkeley: University of California Press, 1972). Part 1, "The Movement"; part 2, "The Society." See especially chapter 12, "The Military and Politics."

[35] David Morell, "Alternatives to Military Rule in Thailand," *Armed Forces and Society* 1 (Spring 1975): 287–301.

civilian competitive politics, had at their disposal very strong paramilitary forces indispensable for the degree of regime consolidation that has come to exist. The civilian authoritarian regime in Ceylon has shown its viability by using its combined military and paramilitary forces to repress the major and carefully executed student-based revolt that involved extensive external support from North Korea. Malaysian competitive politics operates through an effective paramilitary force that contains dissident minority groupings. Singapore has comparable agencies and institutions. From our perspective, the rise of the paramilitary in both India and the Philippines provides striking examples of the role of coercive agencies. In both, heavy reliance on paramilitary forces creates the preconditions for more extensive actual and potential involvement of the military in domestic politics. In the Philippines the constabulary played a decisive role in suppressing the Communist-dominated revolt after World War II and has been continuously engaged in policing the dissident Moslem group. The strength and organization of the constabulary enabled President Marcos to declare martial law in 1972.

Although the data are scarce, India supplies a vivid example of the relationship among the internal political developments, the growth of the paramilitary units, and the patterns of coercion. The Public Accounts Committee of the Indian Parliament, in a report in October 1974, concluded that government expenditures for paramilitary forces had increased by 52 times in the twenty-four years since 1950 and had doubled in the five years preceding 1974.[36]

The structures of the national police forces and paramilitary agencies in India are very complicated and contain numerous separate but overlapping elements. There are three main forces. First, after the defeat of the Indian army by China, a special border security force was established. Its purpose was to relieve

[36] Reported in *The New York Times*, 24 October 1974; for an analysis of the Indian military, see Stephen P. Cohen, *The Indian Army: Its Contributions to the Development of a Nation* (Berkeley: University of California Press, 1971).

the Indian army of the day-to-day policing of the northern frontier; this frontier paramilitary force has been enlarged to operate on the Pakistan and Bangladesh borders. Then there is the Central Reserve Police, comparable to the National Guard in the United States. It reportedly comprises 60 battalions with a total of 54,000 men, and it has been used to control civil agitations in various provinces. The third force is the Central Industrial Force, which protects government property and is reported to have 15,000 men. In 1974–75, the central government's allocation for police and paramilitary forces was approximately $200 million; its expenditures for health were $115 million, and for education, $74 million.

The central government of India has also increased the number of personnel engaged in internal intelligence and surveillance tasks. When the prime minister declared a state of emergency in June 1975, these security officers responded with a higher level of effectiveness than was typical of most governmental agencies. The paramilitary forces were able rapidly to control and disperse all forms of organized and public resistance, at least for the moment.

Among those nations which have experienced successful military coups in the Asia region, the political dynamics of military interventionism is operative, although the consequences hardly ensure economic or social progress. The military regimes in the Asia region that have achieved some degree of consolidation include Burma, Indonesia, and South Korea; Afghanistan appears to be another. In each, paramilitary units or their equivalents are essential. In Burma, the military regime has persisted by skillful international neutrality—but at the cost of economic deterioration and loss of control of important sections of the hinterland. In Indonesia, after prolonged activist and interventionist aspirations by Sukarno and the attempted destruction of the military leadership by Communists, the Suharto regime has begun to display a search for a new political equilibrium. The measure of regime consolidation that had been achieved by the end of 1975 involves very controlled efforts to generate a basis of political legitimacy and civilian political participation.

The government of South Korea conforms to parts of the Ataturk model of a military regime explicitly concerned with social and economic progress, and on the basis of its internal success it has sought to transform itself into an elected political party.[37] Despite the measure of political effectiveness and legitimacy achieved by three relatively free elections, international tensions have led the Park regime to rely extensively on repressive measures. Rather than building up an extensive paramilitary force, the Park regime employs local police units specially trained for riot control, and regular military units designed for internal security functions, in particular the Seoul Military Command, which is in the capital and under General Park's immediate overview. In turn, the Korean CIA has repeatedly intervened to intimidate and repress leaders of the political opposition. Pakistan displayed the initial stages of a military regime with a moderate type of administration under General Ayoub Khan. Over time, Pakistan appeared disposed toward a more interventionist phase until the military regime collapsed because of its defeat in the 1969 Indo-Pakistan war. Nepal remains untouched by its politico-military elements. Bangladesh was launched with an authoritarian civilian regime; but in 1975 it had its first military coup.

Thus, in the Asia region there are special examples that do not conform to the natural history of sociopolitical movements—North Korea, Taiwan, Thailand. However, a larger number of nations have followed political transformation as a result of direct military intervention—Afghanistan, Burma, Indonesia, South Korea. In addition, another important group have civilian regimes that rely heavily on paramilitary institutions—Ceylon, India, and the Philippines. These regimes may or may not pass through a period of

[37] C. I. Eugene Kim, "Transition from Military Rule: The Case of South Korea," *Armed Forces and Society* 1 (Spring 1975): 302–16; Jae Souk Sohn, "Political Dominance and Political Fortune: The Role of the Military in the Republic of Korea," in Henry Bienen, ed., *The Military Intervenes* (New York: Russell Sage Foundation, 1968), pp. 103–26.

military rule, but they are engaged in political transformations that have given them the apparatus for more coercive control.

Of the twenty-six nations we included in Sub-Sahara Africa, the remaining example of traditional and personal authoritarian control was eliminated when the Lion of Judah was deposed in 1974. Political independence came last to Sub-Sahara Africa, and colonial rule had gone far in undermining traditional leadership. The region has the features of a historical and ecological entity—despite enormous diversity—and has displayed a pattern of diffusion of military intervention. One can almost speak of Francophone and Anglophone sequences of diffusion. In the Francophone area, the sequence started soon after the restructuring of France's relations with black Africa in 1960. In the British areas, the process was delayed.

Nine of the twenty-six nation-states have not experienced a successful military coup. The frequency of military coups reached a high point in 1965–69 and has decreased sharply thereafter, reflecting an increase in stability. The nine nations that have not had successful military coups in Sub-Sahara Africa belong to two groups. One comprises those nations where charismatic or strong leaders maintain their civil regimes by their personal presence and a limited reliance on paramilitary agencies: Cameroon, Ivory Coast, Kenya, Malawi, Mauritania, and Senegal. These nations have not yet been tested by a struggle for succession, and their militaries have the potential for direct takeover. The other group includes those nations in which civilian leaders have taken active steps to control the armed forces, that is, control them over the short run: Liberia, Guinea, Tanzania, and Ghana. In Liberia a rightist regime has drastically reduced the viability and scope of the military and used political surveillance extensively. In Guinea and Tanzania there has been a leftist outlook in civilian political control. The national leaders in these two countries are explicitly committed to political control over the military by some form of "popular" political devices, including a balancing of the military and politicized paramilitary forces. Ghana illustrates the difficulty of one-party political control of the military even when the party develops its own political thugs and "workers' militia." Thus Ghana has emerged as the image and reality of a military regime designed to thwart a leftist or "mass" party regime.

It would be mistaken to conclude that the military coups that have occurred in Sub-Sahara Africa are essentially no more than personalistic power struggles without features of patterned intent. No doubt this has been true in varying degree, and even predominately in specific coups, especially in the smaller states of Francophone Africa. The very need to collect and allocate resources to support the military establishment itself, however, leads to pressure for some organizational and societal transformation. In this region there are military regimes that are not engaged merely in maintaining the existing political balance, although their accomplishments are greatly limited and distorted by extensive personal corruption. The military leadership brought into power by the second coup in Ghana was more interventionist than the first, even though its goals were most modest. The military-based regime in Zaire has ruled with heavy reliance on its paramilitary forces, but it has gradually sought to develop a more activist program and has thus, after a period of instability, produced a relatively consolidated regime. In Nigeria increased resources for oil exploration are crucial for the military regime, but again the leaders of the 1975 coup had reformist aspirations.[38] The most radical professed policies are found in the declarations and initial actions of the officers and noncommissioned officers engaged in ending the Ethiopian monarchy.[39]

Thus, in summary, Sub-Sahara Africa as a region has lagged behind in the emergence of more consolidated regimes such as those of the Middle East. However, the natural history of these

[38] For an analysis of the social-political and institutional bases of the coups in Nigeria, see Robin Luckham, *The Nigerian Military: A Socological Analysis of Authority and Revolt, 1960–1967* (Cambridge: Cambridge University Press, 1971).

[39] For the background of the military involvement in Ethiopia, see Donald N. Levine, "The Military in Ethiopian Politics: Capabilities and Constants," in Bienen, *The Military Intervenes*, pp. 5–34.

military regimes reflects both an element of realism among military leaders and a measure of increased stability derived from their bureaucracies, especially their paramilitary agencies.

In South America there has been a high frequency of successful military coups throughout the entire period from 1945 to 1975. With the suspension of the legislature in Uruguay in 1973, there is now no country in South America that has been exempt from a successful military coup. On first examination, the data show no evidence of a decreasing trend, and therefore no evidence of an increase in regime consolidation. This steady occurrence of successful military coups reflects the strong persistence of the conventional South American military coup designed to maintain or adjust the existing internal political balance. While most successful coups have been of this variety, there have been some interventionist and prolonged military efforts with greater potentials for regime consolidation.

As mentioned earlier, the Brazilian coup of 1964 has come to be regarded as the first new-styled coup in South America. While it was executed by conventionally motivated officers, it developed its own dynamics and produced commitment to and policies of economic growth and societal transformation.[40] The more activist posture of its military leaders was a response to increased social unrest and the inability of the existing political and administrative apparatus to function effectively. By 1968–69 the Brazilian military claimed success in attaining its objectives but did not indicate any clear intent to create a civilian regime. It ruled with repressive techniques and with much more coercion than appeared necessary to the outside observer. The striking feature in Brazil —as in Iran—is that the activist posture arose from a rightist orientation.

In contrast to developments in Brazil, in Argentina the tactics of the military did not produce a unified or effective military interventionism. Differences in internal social structure must be

[40] Alfred Stepan, *The Military in Politics: Changing Patterns in Brazil* (Princeton, N. J.: Princeton University Press, 1971).

taken into account, as well as the pressure of a large Peronist segment of the Argentinian population that reduced the options available to the military. Moreover, the military in Argentina did not display high internal cohesion. It is tempting to contrast the Brazilian and Argentine coups, but such a comparison is difficult because of differences in the size and cultural composition of the two countries. Nevertheless the Argentine coup must be judged as a case of military intervention which, though it had activist overtones, had not, as of 1975, followed a natural history leading toward regime consolidation.

Chile and Uruguay are two additional examples of prolonged military interventionism generated from a rightist orientation, while Peru represents a leftist posture. The Chilean military was one of the few in South America that had accepted civilian control but also perceived itself as the "protector" of the constitution. The threat of rural unrest that the paramilitary units were unable to contain, plus the efforts of the left Socialist party to create a socialist regime, nevertheless led the military, albeit reluctantly, to a direct assumption of power. The Chilean military has consequently embarked on activist programs influenced by Brazilian examples.

Uruguay also, with its strong tradition of civilian control and long welfare-state experience, had a military that only reluctantly and only to a limited extent accepted prolonged intervention. Again, the failure of the Uruguayan paramilitary agencies to contain both urban and rural violence has led to expanded intervention by the army. In the process, the army "discovered" the need for social reform and in 1973 suspended parliament in order to initiate and implement the reforms and reconstruction it believed necessary but which have been slowly implemented.

In Peru the failure of conventional politics led to the emergence of a leftist ideology in military circles, especially in the higher military schools. The military coup in 1968 resulted in a radical military junta whose members did not think of themselves as a caretaker or brief transitional government. This military junta has been able to remain in power since 1968 and has produced some regime stability, although there is great popular distrust, and its efforts to develop civilian linkages have not been notably successful. It does appear that Argentina, Chile, Peru, and Uruguay have experienced an element of diffusion. In each of these countries, however, the military has adapted to its immediate political environment.

Venezuela and Colombia are two South American nations where military regimes have given way to civilian rule. In Venezuela, because of the resources generated by oil extraction, the degree of consolidation has been marked. In Colombia the elaborate efforts of civilian political leaders led to an electoral pact that has provided a transitional period, but one that has not ensured the long-term survival of a civilian regime. The Colombian military has had long experience in a limited form of intervention because of its efforts to suppress the fratricidal violence of the rural areas. In fact, this role of the military—which started in the 1950s—represents an early forerunner of the tactics of military activism in South America.

Thus in summary one should not focus only on the continued numerical frequency of successful military coups in South America. There is an important concentration of nation-states that have had the new type of intervention coup and others that are potential candidates for such coups. Where military coups of this variety have taken place, the natural history of a sociopolitical movement has come into play, with degrees of increased regime consolidation.

Central America, at a much slower pace, has followed the emerging pattern of South America. From 1945 to 1975 the total number of successful military coups has declined sharply. Most of them have been of the conventional type, but prolonged military takeovers with active interventionist goals have occurred. Nicaragua experienced an early military intervention that became fairly activist as a result of encouragement and extensive support from the United States. More clearly activist have been the military interventions in Guatemala in March 1963 and in Honduras in April 1975.

CONCLUSIONS

The available data indicate that in the developing nations there has been a dramatic increase in the size of the agencies of internal coercion, especially the paramilitary units. This trend has been conspicuous from 1965 to 1975. There is every reason to believe that the increase in size has in general been accompanied by greater effectiveness of these coercive units. Likewise, there has been a discernible if fragile trend toward regime persistence and consolidation under military rule. However, there is no reason to claim that the increased political persistence of military regimes is a result of either their effectiveness or their lack of effectiveness in dealing with matters of economic productivity.

The idea of a natural history of the sociopolitical movement helps clarify the societal transformation in the new nations after 1945 and in Latin America after 1960. The natural history perspective focuses on the ability of leaders to remain in power; it highlights the shift in an elite strategy from limited reform to marked interventionist aspirations and then to the emergence of a Thermidor—or of more pragmatic consolidation. For each of the periods, one must keep in mind the capability and effectiveness of the coercive agencies available to the elite—not only the regular armed forces but also the paramilitary forces. During the period of initial transition or mild reform, the level of actual coercion has been indeed limited. During the period of intense interventionism, these nations have not displayed the format of massive coercion associated with totalitarian states. Only in the subsequent phase of regime consolidation have the coercive agencies demonstrated their increased influence. At best, on a case-by-case basis, this perspective is applicable to no more than a majority of the developing nations, especially to the larger ones. This type of exploration at least undermines the view of chronic, or even random, instability. No doubt there are structural and cultural factors that affect the tempo, extent, and consequences of the natural history pattern, but they do not emerge simply or clearly. There are certainly regional patterns, since to lump the developing nations of the world in one statistical sample is to distort the available materials.

Moreover, the case-by-case assessment highlights the fact that the politics and repressive mechanisms of the developing nations under the various forms of military rule, including those regimes that aspire to extensive sociopolitical change, are generally not those of a totalitarian state. The seizure of power by military groups results in a wide variety of patterns of civilian participation, as new but constricted political arrangements come into being. Even in those rare nations where all active organized opposition groups are suspended, a network of informal alliances and tacit mechanisms of group representation operates.

Again and again, one is struck by the efforts of military regimes and their political leaders to search for and experiment with acceptable forms of civilian involvement. The devices range from the use of former political leaders and high civil servants in the cabinet structure in Nigeria, to experiments with local councils in the Sudan, and to explicit coalitions with certain political factions in Indonesia.

Totalitarian regimes present themselves as perpetual ruling bodies. While military regimes are hardly prone to withdraw from power, many are prepared and almost required to search for new mechanisms of political rule and legitimacy. It is as if they had read the more trenchant academic literature on the developing nations—which they have not—and were taking seriously the observations about the necessity to create political organizations and machinery through which they can rule without any escalation of force and coercion.

We are dealing not only with the persistent pressure of civilian leaders and civilian groups to enter and participate in politics but also with the internal dynamics and self-consciousness of the military regime in its different formats. Military regimes vary from the format of a single dominant personality to a junta that may comprise as many as several hundred members. But broadly speaking, military regimes need to maintain the organizational cohesion and unity of their central armed forces. The most direct approach is to limit the day-to-day direct involvement of military personnel in the political and administrative arenas. The need to satisfy the material interests of the military serves as the most profound barrier to curbing such involvement. Organized or informal political surveillance becomes the tool for preventing countercoups, although overt efforts to build coalitions with the leaders of operating military units are probably the more important mechanism of regime consolidation.

A contemporary military regime with interventionist goals searches for an element of legitimacy and often presents itself with an admixture of military and civilian symbols. The degree of civilianization can be superficial—the chief military officer drops his military title and uniform and displays traditional regalia. On the other hand, it may be as thoroughgoing as the Ataturk model, involving the creation of a full-fledged civilian-oriented political party, as in South Korea. The factors that predispose a military regime toward civilianization are only dimly discernible as yet, but they appear to be of the voluntaristic variety—the skill of key leaders, ideological and career experiences, and so forth.[41]

These observations hardly lead to the conclusion that there is no difference, in the developing nations, between a military regime and a civilian one in political formula and coercive tactics. For longer or shorter periods, most developing nations are ruled by interventionist military regimes. My earlier assessment that there are inherent limitations on a military regime's capacity for political rule need not be altered in the light of the events of 1965–75. Military regimes have developed strong coercive instrumen-

[41] S. Finer offers the argument that the more developed a political culture, the less likely a military coup. This is essentially a tautology; when it is applied on a time series basis rather than a cross-sectional basis, there is little empirical support for this idea. S. E. Finer, *The Man on Horseback, 1974: Military Regimes* (London: Penguin, 1974).

talities that contribute to their longevity. They have passed through, in varying tempos and degrees, the natural history of sociopolitical movements, so that their goals and aspirations have become more circumscribed; but since they have not as yet drifted into becoming fully repressive regimes of the totalitarian type, civilian alliances and linkages with civilian groups under military regimes are essential features in their performance and their long-term influences. I still maintain that the most successful military regimes—if one can use this term—are, or will be in the long run, those that are able to share political power with or even transform themselves into more civilian-based political institutions.

II. THE MILITARY IN THE POLITICAL DEVELOPMENT OF NEW NATIONS

1. THE STRATEGY OF COMPARATIVE ANALYSIS

In the comparative study of new nations, two different questions can be asked about the role of the military in political change. First, what characteristics of the military establishment of a new nation facilitate its involvement in domestic politics? Second, what are the capacities of the military to supply effective political leadership for a new nation striving for rapid economic development and social modernization?

These two questions seem to generate very similar answers. Those organizational and professional qualities which make it possible for the military of a new nation to accumulate political power, and even to take over political power, are the same as those which limit its ability to rule effectively. Thus, once political power has been achieved, the military must develop mass political organizations of a civilian type, or it must work out viable relations with civilian political groups. In short, while it is relatively easy for the military to seize power in a new nation, it is much more difficult for it to govern.

Social science literature is rich in its analysis of the social, economic, and political conditions of new nations which weaken parliamentary institutions and civilian political organizations and thereby increase the possibility of military intervention. It is the purpose of this essay, however, to explore civil-military relations from the point of view of the internal social organization of the military, which conditions its political capacities. This includes the dimensions of organizational format, skill structure and career lines, social recruitment and education, and professional and political ideology, as well as cohesion and cleavage.

The focus of this study can be stated alternatively in comparative terms. First, there is the comparative analysis of the military profession in old nations and new ones. Why are military officers of new nations, as compared with those in Western industrialized societies, more influential in domestic politics? Clearly, the social structure of their countries predisposes them to political activism. But, to what extent can this greater involvement be accounted for by particular sociological characteristics of the military profession? Second, comparative analysis deals with variations in the extent and form of military involvement in domestic politics from country to country. The capacity to act in politics is hardly a constant. What characteristics of the military profession help account for differences in civil-military relations in different new nations?

CIVIL-MILITARY RELATIONS: OLD NATIONS AND NEW

Experience in civil-military relations in different Western nation-states has hardly been uniform. But where mass democracy has emerged, the intervention of the military establishment in domestic politics has become limited, and its influence is felt mainly in the conduct of foreign affairs and defense policies. Similarly, in one-party Communist regimes, the military has been neutralized in its internal political power, although, as in mass democratic states, it remains an important agent in influencing foreign affairs.

As a basis for comparing industrialized states with new nations, it is possible to identify three models of political-military or civilian-military relations — aristocratic, democratic, and totalitarian.[1] It seems appropriate to speak of the aristocratic model of political-military elite structure as a composite pattern of Western European powers before industrialism began to have its full impact.[2] There is a comprehensive hierarchy in the aristocratic model which delineates both the source of authority and the prestige of any member of the military elite. The low specialization of the military profession makes it possible for the political elite to supply the bulk of necessary leadership for the military establishment. The classic pattern is exemplified by the aristocratic family which supplies one son to politics and one to the military. Birth, family connections, and common ideology insure that the military will embody the ideology of dominant groups in society. Political control is civilian control, because there is an identity of interest between aristocratic and military groups. The military is responsible because it is a part of the government and, as such, develops a conservative political outlook.

In contrast to the aristocratic model stands the democratic one. Under the democratic model, civilian and military elites are sharply differentiated. Civilian-political elites exercise control over the military through a formal set of rules, which specify the functions of the military and the conditions under which the military may exercise its power. In particular, these rules exclude the military from involvement in domestic partisan politics. Military personnel are professionals in the employ of the state, and their careers are distinct from civilian careers. In fact, being a professional soldier is incompatible with holding any other significant social or political role. Military leaders obey the government because they accept the basic national and political goals of a democracy, and because it is their duty and their profession to fight. Professional ethics, as well as democratic parliamentary institutions, guarantee civilian political supremacy.

The democratic model is not a historical reality but an objective of political policy. Elements of the democratic model have been

[1] For a fuller exposition of these models, see Appendix.
[2] Alfred Vagts, *The History of Militarism* (New York: W. W. Norton, 1937).

achieved only in certain Western industrialized countries, since it
requires viable parliamentary institutions and broad social consensus about the ends of government. The democratic model assumes
that military leaders can be strongly motivated by professional
ethics, and this objective is most difficult to achieve during periods
of sustained conflict.

In the absence of a development toward the democratic model,
historical change tends to replace the aristocratic model with a
totalitarian one.[3] The totalitarian model, as it developed in Germany, in Russia, and, to a lesser degree, in Italy, rests on political
control of the military by a centralized and authoritarian one-party
political system. In part, the military supports the political elite
because the totalitarian party places extensive resources at its
control. The revolutionary elite, bedecked with paramilitary symbols, is dedicated to revitalizing the military. The expanded military profession is given an area of professional competence within
the strategic goals of the totalitarian party. Political control of the
totalitarian variety is enforced by the secret police, by infiltration
of party members into the military hierarchy, by the party's arming its own military units, and by control of the system of officer
selection. While he helps fashion defense policy, the organizational independence of the professional officer is weakened and he
is eliminated from domestic politics.

But neither the democratic nor the totalitarian model adequately serves to describe civil-military relations in the "typical"
new nation. These models are not applicable because the military
has wider involvement in domestic economic, social, and political
change.[4] Fundamentally, this derives from the weakness of civilian

[3] Hans Speier, *War and the Social Order: Papers in Political Sociology*
(New York: G. W. Stewart, 1952.)
[4] Harold Lasswell's concept of the "garrison state" is more applicable
(see "The Garrison State and Specialist on Violence," *American Journal of
Sociology*, XLVI [January, 1941], 455–68). The garrison state is a model
for describing the weakening of civil supremacy, especially in democratic
states, because of the "permanent" threat of mass warfare. While the end
result of the garrison state approximates aspects of the totalitarian state,
the garrison state has a different natural history. It is, however, not the direct
domination of politics by the military. Since modern industrial nations cannot

political institutions, as described by Edward Shils [5] and others. It is the result of the sheer quantity of resources that the military establishment, in comparison with other bureaucratic institutions and professional groups, has been able to accumulate.

In the second half of the twentieth century, the processes of government are so complex, even in the new nations, and the pressures of mass political movements are so intense, that personal military dictators are outmoded, or at best transitional devices. Therefore, models for describing the political activities of the military in new nations during the last fifteen years range from performing the minimal governmental functions essential for any nation-state to that of constituting themselves as the exclusive governing political group. For the purposes of analyzing the military in the political development of new nations, five types of civil-military relations can be identified: (1) authoritarian-personal control, (2) authoritarian-mass party, (3) democratic competitive and semi-competitive systems, (4) civil-military coalition, and (5) military oligarchy. (See Table 1, where the new nations of this study are classified into these categories as of January, 1963).

Although the first three differ markedly in the form of internal political control, they have the common feature that the military's involvement in domestic politics is at the minimal level; it is therefore possible to describe its activities as limited to the mark of sovereignty. As such, the officer corps is not involved in domestic partisan politics but functions as an institution symbolizing the independent and legitimate sovereignty of the new nation,

---

be ruled merely by the political domination of a single small leadership bloc, the garrison state is not a throwback to a military dictatorship. It is the end result of the growth of power by the military elite under conditions of prolonged international tension. The garrison state is a new pattern of coalition in which military groups, directly and indirectly, wield unprecedented amounts of political and administrative power. The military retains its organizational independence provided that it makes appropriate alliances with civil political factions. Since the garrison state requires a highly developed industrial base, the concept is not directly applicable to the new nations.

[5] Edward A. Shils, *Political Development in the New States* (The Hague: Mouton & Co., 1962).

both at home and abroad. The mark of sovereignty includes the military's contribution to internal law and order and to the policing of the nation's borders. Since new nations are immediately involved in international relations, the military is required as a token force for United Nations operations and regional security affairs.

There are alternative political formats by which the military may be limited to the role of a mark of sovereignty. The first is an authoritarian regime, which may be based on personal and traditional power, as in Ethiopia, or it may be a newly developed personal autocracy, as in South Vietnam. This is the (1) *authoritarian-personal* type of civil-military control and is likely to be found in nations just beginning the process of modernization (see Table 1). In a few countries, the military is no more than a mark of sovereignty and is excluded from domestic politics by the power of civilian authoritarian political power; for example, in Ghana, Mali, and Guinea. Such authoritarian power may be rooted in a one-party state, under strong personal leadership, without parliamentary institutions. This type of civil-military relations can be labeled (2) *authoritarian-mass party* control. In these states, both the civilian police and paramilitary institutions operate as counterweights to the military, which is small and not yet fully expanded. Elsewhere the military has a limited role because it is organizationally undeveloped, or, as in the case of some ex-French West African countries, the Africanization of the officer corps is not yet completed. On the other hand, in a few nations, e.g., in Nigeria, Malaya, and India, the military is limited to these functions because of the strength of competitive democratic institutions, and the pattern of civil-military relations which is based on civilian control can be called (3) *democratic-competitive*. In the democratic-competitive system, which must be defined to include semicompetitive systems, as in Tunisia and Morocco, civilian supremacy operates to limit the role of the military in part because colonial traditions implanted a strong sense of self-restraint on the military. In these countries, there are competing civilian institutions and power groups, as well as a mass political party which dominates domestic politics but permits a measure of political competition.

When the military expands its political activity and becomes a political bloc, the civilian leadership remains in power only because of the military's passive assent or active assistance. The extent of political competition decreases; and it is appropriate to describe such a pattern as a (4) *civil-military coalition*, because of the crucial role of the armed forces. Here the military serves as an active political bloc in its support of civilian parties and other bureaucratic power groups. The civilian group is in power because of the assistance of the military. Indonesia provides an example of such political intervention. The military may act as an informal, or even explicit, umpire between competing political parties and political groups as it does in, for example, Turkey. The military may, at this level, be forced to establish a caretaker government, with a view to returning power to civilian political groups. Such were the intention and practice of the first Burmese military government and the intention of Pakistani military leaders. These alliances and caretaker governments are unstable; they frequently lead to a third and wider level of involvement, where the military sets itself up as the political ruling group as in, for example, Thailand, Egypt, and Sudan. The result is a (5) *military oligarchy*, because for a limited time, at least, the political initiative passes to the military. When an actual takeover occurs and the military becomes the ruling group, civilian political activity is transformed, constricted, and repressed.

But it is our basic assumption that the military operates at each level of political intervention, including the takeover of political power, as incomplete agents of political change. Thus, an additional type of civil-military relations, in part hypothetical, and to some degree actually emerging, must be postulated. After "takeover," the military regime can begin to recognize the task of supplying national political leaders. At this level, the military recognizes the needs for a mass political base. It seeks to develop a broader political apparatus, either with its own personnel, under their direct supervision, or through a system of alliances with civilians. Trends in this direction already can be noted in Egypt, South Korea, and, to a lesser extent, in Pakistan.

There is no evolutionary process by which a new nation passes from one level of intervention to another, although a pattern of broadening commitments is discernible. It may well be possible for the military in some nations to limit its intervention to that of an active political bloc, along with other groups, and avoid becoming the political ruling group. But the task remains of clarifying the contributions of professional military to these different patterns of domestic politics, since these types give more concrete meaning to the forms of militarism in the new nations.

HISTORICAL AND ECONOMIC DIMENSIONS

The initial step in the comparative analysis of the military in the political development of new nations is to examine, even briefly, the historical and economic factors which fashioned these military establishments. That the objects of our analysis are highly diverse is an obvious fact, but one which complicates our task. The population range of new nations in 1960 varied from India with over 400 million to Gabon with less than 0.5 million. *The United Nations Demographic Yearbook* for 1960 lists, for Africa and Asia, sixty-four political reporting units with a population of over 1 million inhabitants, if China, Taiwan, Japan, and the Union of South Africa are excluded as special cases. From a population basis, is there a minimum level required to support, even with outside assistance, a military establishment which has internal political consequences? The level of 1 million population seems to include all the smaller nations with politically relevant military establishments, even though some of these establishments may be dependent on foreign assistance.

All these sixty-four political reporting units have armed forces, although some as yet have not developed self-contained military establishments with indigenous officers. Ten of them were at that time still colonial dependencies, two are Soviet bloc allies (North Korea and North Vietnam), and one is semi-internationalized (Laos), with the result that the analysis is limited to fifty-one nations for comparative purposes.[6] (See Table 1 for a list of these countries and some basic characteristics of their armed forces.)

For comparative purposes, historical background involves two crucial aspects: differences in cultural-geographical area and variation in the natural history of the armed forces. The armed forces of new nations can be grouped into three vast cultural-geographical areas which reflect pervasive political and underlying social structural differences: South and Southeast Asia, the Middle East and North Africa, and Sub-Sahara Africa. Obviously, differences within each of these areas are marked, but in each there is a historical unity based on the aftermath of colonial rule.

In South and Southeast Asia, indigenous military institutions, with the exception of those of Thailand, were eliminated, transformed, or replaced by the metropolitan powers. Despite different forms of political rule and economic organization, South and Southeast Asia were the areas of maximum impact of colonial rule. Colonial rule rested on military force, but colonialism is not a form of direct military government. Japanese occupation in many areas did introduce military intervention in domestic politics for a brief but sometimes decisive period. However, the armies that were left behind by the colonial regimes or that came into being during World War II had to be articulated with civilian political institutions. The nations of this area emerged from a historical tradition of colonial rule and not of military rule. Their political heritage — except for the impact of the Japanese occupation — was not that of the military in politics.

[6] South Korea and South Vietnam were included, since in these countries the military is active in the domestic political life of the nation despite the presence of United Nations and American military formations. Although the armed forces of the Congo (Leopoldville) disintegrated after liberation, that country is included because United Nations assistance has reconstructed it to the point where it is of some political importance. The African nations of the so-called French community are also included, despite their defense treaty with France.

TABLE 6

Basic Data on Armed Forces of New Nations

Country	Population (Millions)	Date of Independence	Civil-Military Model	Political Role	Origin of Armed Forces
SOUTH AND SOUTHEAST ASIA					
India	402,600	1947	Democratic-competitive	Mark of sovereignty	Ex-colonial
Indonesia	90,000	1949	Civil-military coalition	Political bloc	National liberation °
Philippines	24,718	1946	Democratic-competitive	Mark of sovereignty	Ex-colonial
South Korea	23,848	1945	Military oligarchy	Political ruling group	Post-liberation °
Thailand	21,881	Non-col.	Military oligarchy	Political ruling group	Non-colonial
Burma	20,457	1948	Military oligarchy	Political ruling group	National liberation
South Vietnam	13,790	1954	Authoritarian-personal control	Mark of sovereignty	Ex-colonial†
Afghanistan	13,150	Non-col.	Authoritarian-personal control	Mark of sovereignty	Non-colonial
Ceylon	9,612	1948	Democratic competitive	Mark of sovereignty	Ex-colonial
Nepal	9,044	1951	Authoritarian-personal control	Mark of sovereignty	Ex-colonial
Malaya	6,698	1957	Democratic-competitive	Mark of sovereignty	Ex-colonial
Cambodia	4,845	1953	Authoritarian-personal control	Mark of sovereignty	Ex-colonial
MIDDLE EAST AND NORTH AFRICA					
Pakistan	86,823	1947	Military oligarchy	Political ruling group	Ex-colonial
Turkey	26,881	Non-col.	Civil-military coalition	Political bloc	Non-colonial
Egypt	25,365	1952	Military oligarchy	Political ruling group	Ex-colonial
Iran	20,457	1945	Civil-military coalition	Political bloc	Non-colonial
Morocco	10,550	1956	Democratic-competitive †	Mark of sovereignty	Ex-colonial§
Algeria	10,930	1962	Civil-military coalition	Political bloc	National liberation
Iraq	6,952	1932	Military oligarchy	Political ruling group	Ex-colonial
Saudi Arabia	6,000 est.	Non-col.	Authoritarian-personal control	Mark of sovereignty	Non-colonial
Yemen	4,500 est.	Non-col.	Military oligarchy	Political ruling group	Non-colonial
Syria	4,539	1946	Civil-military coalition	Political ruling group	Ex-colonial
Tunisia	3,935	1956	Democratic-competitive †	Mark of sovereignty	National liberation
Israel	2,061	1948	Democratic-competitive	Mark of sovereignty	Ex-colonial
Jordan	1,636	1946	Civil-military coalition	Political bloc	Ex-colonial
Lebanon	1,550	1941	Democratic-competitive	Political bloc	Ex-colonial

SUB-SAHARA AFRICA

Nigeria	35,400	1960	Democratic-competitive	Mark of sovereignty	Post-liberation
Ethiopia	21,000	Non-col.	Authoritarian-personal control	Mark of sovereignty	Non-colonial
Congo (Leopoldville)	13,652	1960	Civil-military coalition	Political bloc	Post-liberation
Sudan	10,262	1956	Military oligarchy	Political ruling group	Ex-colonial
Tanganyika	9,238	1962	Democratic-competitive ‡	Mark of sovereignty	Post-liberation
Ghana	6,690	1957	Authoritarian-mass party	Mark of sovereignty	Ex-colonial
Madagascar	5,239	1960	Not classified	Mark of sovereignty	Post-liberation
Mali	4,300	1960	Authoritarian-mass party	Mark of sovereignty	Post-liberation
Upper Volta	3,537	1960	#	Mark of sovereignty	Post-liberation
Cameroun	3,225	1960	#	Mark of sovereignty	Post-liberation
Ivory Coast	3,103	1960	#	Mark of sovereignty	Post-liberation
Guinea	2,727	1958	Authoritarian-mass party	Mark of sovereignty	Post-liberation
Chad	2,730	1960	#	Mark of sovereignty	Post-liberation
Ruanda	2,634	1962	Not classified	Mark of sovereignty	Post-liberation
Niger	2,550	1960	#	Mark of sovereignty	Post-liberation
Senegal	2,550	1960	#	Mark of sovereignty	Post-liberation
Sierra Leóne	2,400	1961	Democratic-competitive ‡	Mark of sovereignty	Ex-colonial
Burundi	2,213	1962	Not classified	Mark of sovereignty	Post-liberation
Dahomey	2,000	1960	#	Mark of sovereignty	Post-liberation
Somali	1,990	1960	Authoritarian personal control	Mark of sovereignty	Post-liberation
Togo	1,642	1960	°°	Mark of sovereignty °°	Post-liberation
Cameroons	1,621	1960	Not classified	Mark of sovereignty	Post-liberation
Liberia	1,500	Non-col.	Authoritarian-personal control	Mark of sovereignty	Post-liberation
Central African Republic	1,185	1960	#	Mark of sovereignty	Post-liberation
Libya	1,172	1951	Authoritarian-personal control	Mark of sovereignty	Post-liberation

* A significant ex-colonial element from the Japanese army is included.
† Ex-colonial cadres from the French period were joined with post-liberation forces.
‡ Civilian control is based on semicompetitive political institutions.
§ An important national liberation component, which served as a guerrila force, is included.
# Not classified as a civil-military model, since the armed forces are not integral groups because of defense treaty with France.
°° Military revolt in 1963 resulted in the army assuming the role of political bloc.
Not classified cases imply either absence of data or indeterminacy of situation because of recent independence.

In the Middle East and North Africa, the indigenous Ottoman tradition and the political heritage of the Ottoman Empire were of political involvement and political rule by military officers. Moreover, the impact of colonial rule — as compared with Southeast Asia — was less extensive and less direct. Although there was warfare and violence, military institutions were not radically transformed but only gradually adapted and accommodated to the influence of modernization. Even after liberation, the modernization and professionalization of the military in many countries of this area had to confront the residues of older officer elements. For the military after national liberation, political involvement was a tradition and not an innovation or exception.

In Sub-Sahara Africa, there is a still different historical tradition. The colonial governments easily destroyed indigenous military institutions, and, by contrast with other colonial areas, the area was relatively demilitarized. The metropolitan governments ruled with tiny colonial armed forces and, except for short periods of warfare during World War I and World War II, did not mobilize military manpower of consequence. Moreover, independence was granted without resort to violence or military force. The new nations of the Sub-Sahara region face the problem of creating new institutions and new traditions because of the very absence of extensive military institutions at the time of independence.

When new nations are classified into the three cultural-geographical areas, marked differences emerge in the contemporary political role of the military that can be linked to these historical trends (see Table 1). The most extensive political involvement is in the Middle East and North Africa, where, of the twelve countries with modern armies of a professional type, the military constitutes the political ruling group or military oligarchy in four. The military is actively involved in civil-military coalitions in six, and in only two is the military limited to a non-partisan (mark of sovereignty) role. For the Asian countries, four armies have politically expanded roles, while the other eight have limited roles. These latter, with the exception of India and the Philippines, are in the smaller countries without competitive political systems. In Africa, most of the new nations have had independence for such a short time that the non-partisan role of the military reflects its limited and primitive resources and the newness of the country.

Another approach to classifying new nations is according to the natural history or origin of the military, which again reflects differing colonial practices and the political conditions of liberation. It is possible to speak of four different types. In the few that never experienced colonial rule, or even indirect rule, the armies were the direct outgrowth of self-managed change of a traditional institution. There are three such military establishments, one in each of the cultural-geographical areas, that can be called *non-colonial* military forces in order to emphasize their continuity with the past: those of Thailand, Turkey, and Ethiopia. Liberia's is a variant of this type. Afghanistan's is also close to this type, because the impact of indirect rule was so limited. Saudi Arabia and Yemen have a military which should be called traditional, because of the personal and non-professional character of military services in these countries.

But most armies in these new nations can be classified as either *ex-colonial* armed forces, armed forces established during the struggle for *national liberation*, or *post-liberation* armies, since they were, in essence, established after independence. In number, the *ex-colonial* armies total sixteen, or about one-third; the armies of *national liberation* are only four, or less than 10 per cent; while the most numerous are the *post-liberation* formations, which add up to twenty-seven, or about half the nations.

These types exist not only because Great Britain had a different set of policies from France and the other colonial powers, but also because the British varied their policies in the three cultural-geographical areas. The ex-colonial army, with a cadre of mod·ernly-trained indigenous officers who were available at the time of independence, is a product of British policy in South and Southeast Asia and to a limited extent also in North Africa. The British objective was to create institutions which ultimately would lead to some form of political autonomy within the imperial system. This meant that there was a very slow but gradual process of developing indigenous officer cadres, where political conditions permitted the British to pursue such policies. By contrast, the French were concerned with the political assimilation of the colonial nations into the French polity. As a result, where the French exercised direct rule, as in Indo-China, they were less interested in developing indigenous officers, although they made extensive use of native enlisted personnel. Since the Dutch, Belgians, Spaniards, and Portuguese assumed that colonial rule would continue indefinitely, they did not take steps to create such officer cadres.

But in parts of the Middle East, the British and French also exercised indirect rule, with the result that ex-colonial armies emerging from such indirect rule often have a different character. In these areas, the colonial powers did not build these armies up anew from the bottom but rather sought to refashion them. As a result, the professional standards were often relatively low and the officer corps was often enmeshed in the politics of traditional groups, as in, e.g., Syria and Iraq. These armies seem to emerge after independence with less internal and professional cohesion. The introduction of Western military values, in particular public service traditions and technocratic perspectives, proceeded much more slowly than in Southeast Asia, where the armies were being fashioned after the European models and where the break with the past was more clear-cut.

Variants of the ex-colonial army include those in Israel, South Korea, and South Vietnam. Since 1936, the British had given de facto recognition to the Jewish defense forces, and cadres of the Israeli army were trained and fought under British command during World War II. The South Korean army, after 1945, was built from Japanese-trained officers, while South Vietnamese forces established after 1955 included personnel who had served under the French.

By contrast, the result of colonial rule in Sub-Sahara Africa produced *post-liberation armies.* While the colonial powers mobilized African manpower during World War I and World War II, the style of colonial rule, even for the British, did not result in the building up of an indigenous professional cadre until just before independence. In these former British colonies, the transfer of power was accompanied by positive steps to develop rapidly all the institutions of a nation-state, including a complete and self-contained armed force. Central police forces were in existence, and there was sufficient political stability so that these very small military establishments could be expanded and the officer corps could be rapidly Africanized from the bottom up. The French pattern has been different in that even after independence there remain important residues of integration with French military institutions. In the former French colonies — except for Mali and Guinea, which have severed political ties and turned to the Soviet bloc for assistance — political leaders have formed mutual military alliances with France, with the result that French officers play a crucial role and Africanization is proceeding very gradually.

The natural history of the origins of the military in new nations is not a very good indicator of political roles after independence. Clearly, military formations born in the struggle for national liberation have maintained wide political involvements. Each of the four armies created as a force of national liberation has expanded its political role. While the post-liberation armies are too new to be effective or tested, the ex-colonial armies are divided, about equally, between those which have remained as instruments of national sovereignty and those which have intervened in domestic politics. In other words, ex-colonial armies, including those with high professional standards built by direct British rule and trained under British traditions, have demonstrated a capacity to assume domestic political responsibilities with rapidity (as in Pakistan and Sudan, for example). Ex-colonial origin hardly insures that the military will limit its role to that of the mark of sovereignty.

Yet, the influence of Western professional forms in inhibiting the political aspirations of the military of new nations is not to be dismissed. When the political behavior of the ex-colonial armies is examined in detail, including the conditions under which they become the ruling political group, there is at least an absence of designed militarism, especially in the case of those armies built up by direct British colonial rule. By "designed militarism" we mean the positive and premeditated intent to intervene in domestic politics and to follow expansionist foreign policies. Prussian militarism is the classic case of designed militarism. Instead, these armies display reactive militarism; their political behavior is in part generated by the weakness of civilian institutions and the direct pressure of civilian groups which seek to co-opt and enlarge the role of the military establishment. Of the sixteen ex-colonial armies, elements of designed militarism with its expansive overtones are to be found only in two Middle Eastern countries, Egypt and Iraq, and in these nations, the consequences of the Israeli wars contribute to this positive militarism. In most of the other countries, the military has been drawn into domestic politics because of the weakness of civilian institutions and the positive pressures by civilian groups to expand its role to meet internal political crises.

Another aspect of historical development is the link between political roles of the military and length of time since independence. Leaving aside the Sub-Sahara countries, because of the recency of their independence, there is an apparent but not profoundly explanatory relation between the length of time that a new nation has been independent and the increased political role of the military. Of the countries in which the military has constituted the political ruling group, all but one have had independence for more than ten years. The same pattern holds for those countries in which the military has expanded to become an active coalition ingredient in the domestic political process. But, for those countries where the military is limited to the mark of sovereignty, there has been no consistent pattern since independence; some are relatively new and some relatively old by the standards of new nations. In short, the chance of political involvement increases year by year after independence, while the contraction of the military's political role remains a highly problematic issue (see Table 1).

An alternative basis for grouping new nations and their military establishments is in terms of demographic and economic measures. First, the range in population and size of the military establishment is indeed marked (see Table 2).[7] The Libyan army of 4,500, composed almost exclusively of infantry troops, is hardly the same type of administrative organization as the Indian defense forces of over 500,000, with the first-line jet planes and naval units. In the top ranks are the three "super-states" among the new nations — India, Indonesia, and Pakistan — which constitutes over 60 per cent of the population of this group of new nations. The second-order countries are the nine nations which can be considered large by new nations' standards, because they have populations of over twenty million. (In Southeast Asia, the Philippines, Thailand, Burma, and South Korea; in the Middle East and North Africa, Turkey, Egypt, and Iran; and in Sub-Sahara Africa, Nigeria and Ethiopia.) In effect, the typical new nation is a small country; of the remaining thirty-nine nations, twenty-one have populations under four million.

Second, while new nations with the most modern technology are likely to have the most efficient military establishments, there is no relationship between per capita gross national product and the size of the military establishment. The size of the military is

[7] Statistics on the military forces of new nations are often not reliable. The materials presented in Table 2 are based on the evaluation and synthesis of a large variety of sources. They represent an effort to arrive at the best possible estimate of the situation as of January, 1963. Special reliance was placed on unpublished data supplied by social scientists who have had direct contact with particular military establishments. In this connection, I wish to acknowledge the assistance of Professors William J. Foltz, Yale University; Arthur T. Porter, the University College of Sierra Leone; P. J. Vatikiotis, University of Indiana; David Wilson, University of California at Los Angeles; Drs. Eric du Dampierre, Centre d'Etudes Sociologiques, and Herbert F. Weiss, Columbia University. Relevant publications include *The Statesman's Year Book* and John J. Johnson, *The Role of the Military in Underdeveloped Countries* (Princeton, N.J.: Princeton University Press, 1962), as well as numerous journalistic sources.

less related to economic base than to total population. In other words, new nations must allocate their resources, and military expenditures are relatively fixed costs. A military establishment appears indispensable, and even the poorest countries are involved in developing a military. (The poorest and least economically developed can create a military establishment with limited modern technology, and they have the advantage of surplus manpower for this purpose.) Nations with larger populations seem to be required to have relatively larger armies — for both domestic and international reasons — and they are forced to allocate resources regardless of their economic position. Thus, investment in the military is hardly the result of disposable capital but is rather a fundamental cost which new nations are prepared to extract, whatever their economic ability to pay.

Third, the costs of a military establishment are, in proportion to per capita income, high for a new nation. In particular, military expenditures take a large portion of the public budget. If a nation spends more than 40 per cent of its public budget, it is classified as in the very high category, and in the high category if the figure is more than 25 per cent (see Table 2). Of course, the official public budget often markedly under-represents military expenditures, which can go unreported or be carried on civilian agency budgets. These expenditures also seem to be rising.

The next step is to explore whether there is any relationship between economic development or its absence and the political role of the military in new nations. The results again are mainly negative. Students of comparative politics have offered the proposition that there is a positive association between economic development and democratic political competitiveness. By inference, the more economically developed a new nation is, the less likely it is that the military could hinder the competitive process in politics.

S. M. Lipset made use of selected indices of economic development to compare Western European and Latin American democracies as a basis for testing this hypothesis concerning the positive association between economic development and political competitiveness.[8] James Coleman employed the same type of analysis for the new nations of Asia, the Middle East, and Africa and concluded that "the major hypothesis that economic development and competitiveness are positively correlated is validated when countries are grouped into major differentiating categories of competitiveness and when mean scores of economic development are employed."[9] Coleman presses the analysis further for his group of nations when he adds that "the hypothesis is weakened by negative correlations found when the economic scores and relative competitiveness of individual countries are considered." In the end there are so many countries which are "deviant cases" that the analysis of the deviant cases instead of the original hypothesis about economic development and democratic competitiveness becomes the main and rewarding focus of his analysis.

In any case, this type of analysis appears to have limited relevance for understanding, on a comparative basis, the dynamic relationship between economic development and political forms, especially for the group of fifty-one new nations of this analysis. First, on purely statistical grounds, the support for this basic proposition in the new nations — Asia, North Africa, and Sub-Sahara Africa — is not impressive.[10] Second, in order to avoid a

[8] S. M. Lipset, "Some Social Requisites of Democracy: Economic Development and Political Legitimacy," *American Political Science Review*, LIII (March, 1959), 69–105. For purposes of investigating this proposition, the degrees of competitiveness are limited to three: competitive, semi-competitive, and authoritarian. While the concept of competitiveness involves a political or electoral system, these three degrees of competitiveness can be assumed to be broad enough to encompass alternative institutional arrangements for developing political consensus without recourse to coercion.

[9] James S. Coleman, "The Political Systems of the Developing Areas," *The Politics of the Developing Areas*, ed. Gabriel A. Almond and James S. Coleman (Princeton, N.J.: Princeton University Press, 1960), pp. 532–44. It is possible to accept his request to leave aside questions of "accuracy, comparability, and significance of available economic statistics, as well as the validity of gross judgments regarding the competitive or authoritarian character of political systems."

[10] Coleman himself acknowledges this when he points out that the hypothesis is weakened when the economic scores and relative political competitiveness of individual countries are considered. This is in part due to the

TABLE 7
Basic Data on Armed Forces of New Nations

Country	Population (Millions)	Total* Armed Forces	Total Officers	Per Cent Army	Level of Expenditure (Per Cent)	Economic Development Index†
SOUTH AND SOUTHEAST ASIA						
India	402,600	550,000	...	88	High (25)	2
Indonesia	90,000	350,000	15,000	88	High (30)	2
Philippines	24,718	21,500	...	97	Moderate (16)	2
South Korea	23,848	650,000	...	...	Very high (40)	...
Thailand	21,881	134,000	...	80	Moderate (22)	2
Burma	20,457	149,000‡	5,000	94	High (31)	2
South Vietnam	13,790	205,000	...	96	Very high (45)	2
Afghanistan	13,150	90,000	...	100	Very high (40)	3
Ceylon	9,612	8,881	548	61	Moderate (18)	2
Nepal	9,044	45,000	...	100	High (30)	...
Malaya	6,698	8,000	...	98	High (25)	1
Cambodia	4,845	28,000	2,000	97	Moderate (22)	3
MIDDLE EAST AND NORTH AFRICA						
Pakistan	86,823	260,000	13,000	90	Very high (50)	3
Turkey	26,881	428,500	25,500	88	High (25)	2
Egypt	25,365	80,000	4,000	90	High (24)	1
Iran	20,457	150,000	11,000	96	High (38)	2
Morocco	10,550	35,000	...	94	Moderate (20)	2
Algeria	10,930	65,000	...	100	...	1
Iraq	6,952	60,000	...	...	High (37)	2
Saudi Arabia	6,000 est.	30,000	...	98	...	2
Yemen	4,500 est.	10,000	...	...	...	3 est.
Syria	4,539	45,000	2,000	...	Very high (45)	1
Tunisia	3,935	20,000	...	99	Low (10)	2
Israel	2,061	75,000	...	85	High (34)	1
Jordan	1,636	35,000	1,700	99	Very high (40)	2
Lebanon	1,550	10,800	300	92	Moderate (19)	1

SUB-SAHARA AFRICA

Country						
Nigeria	35,400	7,500	350	97	Low (8)	3
Ethiopia	21,000	30,000	...	97	High (27)	3
Congo (Leopoldville)	13,652	31,600	...	...	...	2
Sudan	10,262	12,000	...	...	Low (12)	3
Tanganyika	9,238	1,000	...	99	Low (3)	3
Ghana	6,690	6,500	...	95	Low (10)	2
Madagascar	5,234	9,000	...	...	...	...
Mali	4,300	3,000	...	...	...	3
Upper Volta	3,537	6,000	...	...	...	3
Cameroun	3,225	2,000	...	...	...	3
Ivory Coast	3,103	1,500	...	...	...	3
Guinea	2,727	2,000	...	...	Low (10)	3
Chad	2,730	1,500	...	...	...	3
Ruanda	2,634	1,000	50	...	...	3
Burunda	2,213	1,000	50	...	...	3
Senegal	2,550	7,000	...	...	...	3
Niger	2,550	2,000	50	...	...	3
Sierra Leone	2,400	1,300	...	...	...	3
Dahomey	2,000	2,000	...	...	...	3
Somali	1,990	6,000	...	...	...	3
Togo	1,642	200§	...	...	...	3
Cameroons	1,621	...	...	...	...	3
Liberia	1,500	5,000	...	...	...	2
Central African Republic	1,185	4,500	...	...	99	3
Libya	1,172	5,000	...	...	...	2

* Includes regular army, navy, and air force personnel who are on active duty and does not include different types of auxiliary reserves, civilian defense forces, or special frontier guards and national police units, which are very large in some countries.

† James Coleman, *op. cit.* (n. 9 above), p. 543.

‡ Includes military police units.

§ Five hundred additional volunteers who served in the French army claim to be members of the armed forces.

mechanical test of the proposition, one would expect that the changes in political competitiveness, since the publication of the data for both Latin America and the new nations of Africa and Asia, would at least be congruent with the basic proposition. This means that those nations high on the economic development index should have moved toward more competitiveness. For Latin America, the trend has been toward less competitiveness, and this trend cannot be directly related to the level of economic development; in some cases, it is inversely related.[11] Of the new nations included in this analysis, since the publication of Coleman's data, seven have also become less competitive. Of these seven, one was at the high economic development category level, three were in the middle, and three were at the lower level of the scale. Such data are not evidence in support of the basic hypothesis.

The weakness of this type of statistical analysis rests in the artificial character of the basic categories of competitive, semi-competitive, and authoritarian groups. To group together as authoritarian the political systems of Afghanistan, where the exercise of power is based upon personal rule, and of Sudan, where the authoritarian regime is the result of a coup d'état by a professional military group, is to obscure comparative analysis.

Thus it becomes more relevant to relate economic development to the more refined five types of civil-military relations of this essay (democratic-competitive, authoritarian-personal, authoritarian-mass party, civil-military coalition, and military oligarchy). Using these categories, there is no basis for asserting that, with

---

fact that a limited number of cases are employed and even a minor redefinition of the universe markedly alters the statistical conclusions. Thus, if, instead of forty-six political units, the fifty-one units of this analysis are utilized, the over-all test of the hypothesis is barely confirmed. This procedure removed political units which still have colonial status and treated each of the eight territories of French West Africa and the four territories of French Equatorial Africa as independent units.

[11] See Dwaine Marvick, "Correlates of Democracy in Latin America," paper delivered at the 57th Annual Meeting of the American Sociological Association, Washington, D.C., September, 1962, for an analysis oriented toward the processes of social and economic change.

higher levels of economic development, there is a movement toward more competitive political systems. In fact, among those
nations with the highest level of economic development, the absence of democratic competitive systems is more noteworthy than
their presence, since competitive systems are concentrated in the
middle level of economic development. But the analysis is not
without meaning if the general hypothesis is abandoned and the
underlying process examined. Authoritarian-personal regimes are
heavily concentrated among the nations with low economic development, for these nations are just embarking on economic
development. These nations have a pattern of civil-military relations which reflects the past, for this is essentially the character
of their authoritarian regimes. Moreover, it is true that there are
no democratic-competitive regimes at the very bottom of the economic ladder. But the economic threshold is rather low for a
democratic-competitive system. The basic conclusion is that, with
higher economic levels, the outcome is as likely as not to be in
the direction of military oligarchy, and perhaps somewhat more
likely. Thus, factors such as natural history of origin, time since
independence, or level of economic development supply, at best,
a limited point of entrance for understanding differences in the
political role of the military in the new nations.

SOCIAL STRUCTURE AND
MILITARY ORGANIZATION

By what intellectual strategy can comparative analysis of the
military be pursued if there is such marked variation between
cultural-geographic area, natural history of origin, and sheer size?
There are two strategies for extending the analysis beyond the
case-study level. One approach is to focus on paired comparisons
of two countries which have important similarities and yet have
emerged with marked differences in civil-military relations: India
and Pakistan, Nigeria and Ghana, Morocco and Indonesia. Despite the complexities, the alternative approach pursued in this
essay is to make some simplifying assumptions and to extend the

range of analysis to a very wide, if not the full, range of new nations.

Basically, the analysis rests on two pervasive assumptions about social structure and military organization. One focuses on the common societal context of the military in new nations; namely, new nations have chosen without exception the goal of modernization. They have embarked in varying degree on programs of managed rapid modernization and social change designed to transform their traditional social structure. Thus, despite differences in national culture and history, from this point of view it is assumed that the military is operating in societies which are confronted with rather similar political, economic, and social requirements. Second, as compared with other institutions and bureaucracies, it is assumed that the military establishment has a variety of common organizational features. These common features condition and limit the capacity of the military profession to exercise political power.

The first assumption raises the question of what is meant when new nations are described as traditional societies in the process of social change. One conception of a traditional society focuses on stability and integration. A traditional society is one with long-standing and relatively unchanged social structure. In this view, the persistence of social and cultural forms is high-lighted. Social changes start and become accelerated with the recent introduction of modern technology, modern administration, and Western values. The process produces increased economic potential, literacy, and urbanism, which corrode traditional forms. Social change is a new process in which there is a passage from traditional society through a transitional phase to modernity. It is a continuation of the "idea of progress" in a non-Western context.[12]

Such a view of social change in the new nations seems inadequate on various grounds. It fails to acknowledge the vast changes

[12] For an exposition of this point of view, see Daniel Lerner, *The Passing of Traditional Society: Modernizing the Middle East* (Glencoe, Ill.: Free Press, 1958).

in economic and demographic growth that were transforming peasant economies even under colonial rule. It seems to assume that these peasant economies, before the advent of colonialism and Western contact, did not have societal-wide political institutions with strong influence on traditional social structure. It seems to imply that traditional societies were merely a collection of villages and communities with no superstructure; but, most important, this view fails to recognize the manner in which traditional values and traditional forms persist during modernization, even though these traditions become modified. Neo-traditional political movements arise which leave their mark on the meaning of "modernity" in non-Western nation-states.

Thus, an alternative view of traditional society seems more appropriate for the task of analyzing the role of the military as an agent of social and political change. In this view, traditional society is a peasant society. Because it is a peasant society, the rate of social change may generally be slow; but peasant societies undergo change, including rapid and drastic change, on occasion, as peasant technology changes. In particular, as peasant societies, new nations were touched by colonialism in the past, and some were completely transformed by colonial agricultural and plantation systems. Since most of the population is engaged in agriculture, the organization of a peasant society rests in the linkage between vast masses of rural population and tiny urban elites who manage the societal institutions. The peasant society is a society in which religious values are paramount. Therefore, an understanding of the sociological implications of traditional religion is essential for understanding the structure of these societies.[13]

The peasant society, like any form of social organization, has its sources of consensus and dissensus. One of the main characteristics of a peasant society is that it can tolerate or accommodate more social dissensus than can a modernized society. The simpler

[13] See Clifford Geertz, *The Religion of Java* (Glencoe, Ill.: Free Press, 1960), for an example of this type of approach to the analysis of peasant society.

level of technology and division of labor requires less consensus and permits more disarticulation. Even more important in this regard, peasant societies have more limited collective aims and goals. As governments, the colonial regimes were political caretakers, concerned with avoiding the development of native political demands. Under colonialism, and under the impact of Western indirect rule, forms of accommodation had to emerge. But the processes of accommodation generally did not increase internal consensus. On the contrary, internal differentiation increased. In all emerging nations, new groups and new contenders for elite power arose who were oriented toward modernization in terms derived from the West. Dissensus increased with the advent of independence, as the governments strove to develop a base of popular support. But these same nations produced social movements which embodied traditional values. In some areas, traditional religious and political values had weakened under colonialism but became strengthened as independence became a reality. The success of these neo-traditional movements varies from country to country, and in the long run they may atrophy under the impact of modernization. But these neo-traditional movements have had significant impact in heightening nationalism. It is popular to think of the military in new nations as technocratic in orientation and as concerned with modernization, but the military is also concerned with legitimate authority and with historical and national traditions. In analyzing its political ideology and political behavior, one cannot overlook the impact of neo-traditionalism on the military.

The second assumption concerning the special organizational character of the military flows from the notion that the goals of an organization supply a meaningful basis for analyzing its bureaucratic structure. In some respects, the contemporary military establishment has the characteristics of any large-scale bureaucracy. But the military establishment — regardless of its societal context — has a unique character because the threat of violence is a permanent reality to its leaders. The results of previous combat and the pressure to prepare for future combat pervade the entire organization. The unique character of the military derives from the requirement that its key members be specialists in the use of violence.

Changing technology creates new patterns of combat and thereby modifies organizational behavior in the military.[14] The more complex the technology of warfare, the narrower are the differences between military and non-military establishments, because more officers have managerial and technical skills applicable to civilian enterprise. Yet, even the most automated military establishment retains an organizational format which reflects the necessities of combat. Since the military establishments of new nations do not have nuclear capabilities, they still bear many essential characteristics of World War II military organization. Because their technology is relatively similar, they have relatively similar organizational features, particularly in their systems of hierarchy, status, and authority. They tend to develop similar procedures of recruitment and training, as well as of internal control, that, in turn, control the capacity of the military to intervene in domestic politics. On the other hand, it is more difficult to isolate internal factors which vary from one military establishment to another and which account for differences in political behavior.

The following illustrative propositions about internal organization are offered to help explain the patterns of political behavior of the military in new nations as compared with industrialized nations, on the basis of available data. They are also designed to throw light on differences among the new nations and on the difficulties which confront the military when it becomes the ruling group and must seek to develop mass political support.

1. *Organizational format.* The capacity of the military establishment in new nations to intervene in domestic politics derives

[14] See Appendix for a fuller discussion of the concepts used in this section.

from its distinctive military format, namely, its control of the instruments of violence; its ethos of public service and national identification; and its skill structure, which combines managerial ability with a heroic posture. (In part, this proposition is designed to help explain the greater initial political capacity of the military in comparison with other civilian groups.)

2. *Skill structure and career lines.* While there has been a trend toward "civilianizing" the military profession, the officer corps in the new nations have important limitations in producing those leadership skills in bargaining and political communication that are required for sustained political leadership. These limitations include the absence of a tradition for dealing with clients and publics outside of the military. (While this proposition applies to both industrialized and new nations, it has particular relevance to new nations because of the relative absence of parliamentary and legal institutions for controlling the military.)

3. *Social recruitment and education.* In the new nations, the military establishment is recruited from the middle and lower-middle classes, drawn mainly from rural areas or hinterlands. In comparison with Western European professional armies, there is a marked absence of a history of feudal domination. As a result, the military profession does not have strong allegiance to an integrated upper class which it accepts as its political leader nor does it have a pervasive conservative outlook. Military education contributed to an innovating outlook toward modernization. (This proposition helps to account for the differences between "army and society" in the new nations and the industrialized ones.)

4. *Professional and political ideology.* While it is impossible to identify a military ideology in the new nations, common ideological themes are found which help to explain the professional officer's political behavior. These include a strong sense of nationalism, a puritanical outlook, acceptance of extensive government control of social and economic change, and a deep distrust of

organized civilian politics. As a result of social background, education, and career experiences, military personnel of the new nations become interested in politics, but they maintain a strong distrust of organized politics and civilian political leaders. (As in the case of social recruitment and education, the analysis of political ideology presents a proposition which contrasts the military of industrialized nations with those of the new nations.)

5. *Social cohesion.* The ability of officers to intervene in domestic politics and produce stable leadership is related to internal social cohesion. The military establishments of new nations differ markedly in their internal social cohesion because of differences in training, indoctrination, operational experience, and intergenerational cleavages. (This proposition relates to differences among the armed forces of the various new nations.)

6. *Political intervention.* The "takeover" of power by the military in new nations has generally followed the collapse of efforts to create democratic-type institutions; the military has tended not to displace the single mass-party authoritarian political regimes. After "takeover," the military regime faces the task of supplying national political leadership and of developing mass support for its programs. While this phase is only emerging, the evidence seems to indicate that, if the military is to succeed in this political goal, it must develop a political apparatus outside of the military establishment but under its direct domination. (Comparative analysis in the case of this proposition is designed to help clarify the conditions under which the military comes to recognize the need of mass political support and is able to develop it.)

In exploring these propositions, efforts were made to overcome limitations in published materials by interviewing research scholars who had had extensive experience in the new nations. These scholars had the opportunity for direct observation of the army officers and the military cultures of new nations, although they did not include such materials in their publications. Students who

have served in these armies were interviewed while they were in
residence in the United States.[15]

[15] Documentation on the armies of new nations is limited. Monographic
studies are available for only a few countries, and these sources stress mainly
the political analysis of civilian institutions. Moreover, some of the best research literature is on countries which are highly special and not broadly
representative of the problems of new nations. When the military is discussed,
there is little concern with organizational problems and sociological aspects
of the profession. The best materials on the contemporary period are in the
form of reports by responsible journalists. One of the most comprehensive
studies is *The Emergence of Modern Turkey*, by Bernard Lewis (London:
Oxford University Press, 1961), which presents the historical background
and transformation of the Turkish army and has general relevance for the
study of new nations. Material on the political sociology of the military is
contained in the volume by Johnson, editor, *The Role of the Military in
Underdeveloped Countries*. The essay in this volume by Edward Shils,
entitled "The Military in the Political Development of the New States,"
extends his well-known analysis of political development in new nations
to the military. See also Morroe Berger, *Military Elites and Social Change:
Egypt since Napoleon*, Research Monograph No. 6, Center for International Studies, Princeton; Majid Khadduri, "The Role of the Military in
Middle East Politics," *American Political Science Review*, June, 1953,
pp. 511–24; Dankwart Rustow, "The Army and the Founding of the Turkish
Republic," *World Politics*, July, 1959, pp. 513–52; Daniel Lerner and Richard
D. Robinson, "Swords and Ploughshares: The Turkish Army as a Moderniz-
ing Force," *World Politics*, October, 1960, pp. 19–44; P. J. Vatikiotis, *The
Egyptian Army in Politics: Pattern for New Nations* (Bloomington: Indiana
University Press, 1961); Richard Butwell, "Civilians and Soldiers in Burma,"
in Robert K. Sahai, *Studies in Asia* (Lincoln: University of Nebraska Press,
1961); Lucien Pye, *Politics, Personality, and National Building* (New Haven:
Yale University Press, 1962); William Gutteridge, *Armed Forces in New
States* (London: Oxford University Press for Institute of Race Relations,
1962); Charles Windle and T. R. Vallance, "Optimizing Military Assistance
Training," *World Politics*, October, 1962, pp. 99–107); and Sydney N. Fisher
(ed.), *The Military in Middle Eastern Society and Politics* (Columbus: Ohio
State University Press, 1963).

2. THE INTERNAL ORGANIZATION OF THE MILITARY

ORGANIZATIONAL FORMAT

The first hypothesis was that the capacity of the military to intervene in domestic politics derived from its distinctive military format; in particular, its control over the instruments of violence. Basically, this proposition does not seek to explain differences in political behavior among the armies of the various new nations. On the contrary, it supplies a basis for understanding the potentials and limitations all these armed forces have for political activity. Moreover, this hypothesis is not self-evident, since the argument has been made directly to the contrary: the non-military functions of the military in new nations are of particular importance in accounting for the military's role as agents of social and political change.[1] The fact that armies in new nations have exercised much of their political influence without violent combat or

[1] See John J. Johnson, *The Role of the Military in Underdeveloped Countries* (Princeton, N.J.: Princeton University Press, 1962), pp. 3 ff.

extensive bloodshed should not obscure the significance of force as the basis from which they exercise their political power. But the argument runs deeper than the sheer use of force — actual or threatened. The underlying rationale is that the organizational format designed to carry out military functions, as well as experience in the "management of violence," is at the root of these armies' ability to intervene politically. The military task is essentially indivisible, as compared to economic and civilian functions, and it contributes thereby to a unified organization with internal cohesion. Likewise, the requirements of preparation for combat and actual combat create an organization with direct political potential, in comparison with economic organizations, because of the underlying ethos and ideology of its leaders.

The technology of the military in the typical new nation maximizes its relevance for intervention in domestic politics. Modern technology has been continuously incorporated into some of these countries by the agency of the military profession since the middle of the nineteenth century. The traditionally independent countries, such as Turkey and Thailand, brought in foreign experts and sent their officers to be trained in Western Europe. Because of the pressure of military operations, colonial armies were often more inclined to technological innovations than the home armies in matters concerning fire-power and the maneuverability of ground forces. It remained, however, for World War II to give the military establishments of new nations their basic technological and organizational format.

The prototype of the new nation's military organization is the World War II infantry battalion. These armies are primarily made up of ground troops, and even the most modern have 85 per cent in the ground forces, with the remainder in the air and naval branches (Table 2 in chap. I). By comparison, in 1960, the United States military forces were 35 per cent ground troops, 34 per cent air force, and 31 per cent naval and marine forces.

Often these infantry battalions have no, or very little, artillery, armor, or logistical support. Even the Israeli army, one of the most effective military organizations by Western standards, is underdeveloped in support units, as was demonstrated in the Sinai campaign. Since World War II, many of these armies have been modernized by an increase of motor vehicles and more effective signal communications, but they remain basically infantry organizations. In varying degrees, the exceptions are Turkey, India, Pakistan, Israel, Egypt, and Indonesia, all of which have modern jet aircraft.

It is because these military establishments are mainly infantry battalions, which can be deployed in urban centers or in rural areas, that they have the maximum potential for involvement in domestic politics. They are in essence a form of super-police. The level of professionalization required for these operations is not great. Naval units, by contrast, are much less effective for domestic political objectives, and only Thailand has produced a group of politically involved naval officers. Air power has potential for domestic intervention, as has been demonstrated in South America where it has been used against ground forces in insurrection. It is more difficult, however, to use an air force against a civil population. Only in Indonesia has the air force developed both a distinctive political orientation, strongly leftist, and direct involvement in domestic politics. But the political importance of an air force unit is likely to increase, in part because of the increased mobility that even a small air establishment can give to ground troops. Sudan, Morocco, and Nigeria have each created the rudiments of an air force especially for border patrol.

The operational experience of new nations' armies is indeed varied, but successful operational activity appears to contribute to internal cohesion. Some formations have extensive experience which contributed to a sense of professional self-esteem and social cohesion. Ex-colonial armies with experience in World War II include India (in Burma and Malaya), Pakistan (in Burma and Malaya), Sudan (in East Africa and Libya), Morocco and Tunisia (in North Africa and Indo-China), and the Philippines (in their own country). To a limited extent, troops from French West

Africa, especially Senegal, fought in North Africa, and the Nigerian and Ghanaian armies had some experience in East Africa and Burma. The cadres of the World War II period have been thinned out by new recruits, but these military experiences left their impact. For post-liberation armies such as the Ghanaian, these experiences have had very limited impact, since, at the time of independence, only 10 per cent of the officers were indigenous. But even the newest armed force has already had some operational experience; the troops of Ruanda have had several successful engagements with Tutsi infiltrators from Kivu (Congo) and Uganda, which have enhanced their cohesion.

A number of new nations have had experience in guerrilla warfare, against both the Japanese and the Western colonial powers (Israel, Morocco, Tunisia, Philippines, Burma, Indonesia, and Algeria). Internal constabulary operations against dissident groups have contributed to the solidarity of the armies of the Philippines, Malaya, and especially Burma, which has had more combat experience than most of the armies of the new nations.[2]

By contrast, the operational experience of the Indonesian military forces during the period of liberation did not unify the military; it developed regional centers of power, especially between the capital region and the hinterlands. Subsequent internal constabulary activities and successful repression of insurrection in the outer islands have not served to overcome this factionalism. A very special case was that of the Force Publique in the Belgian Congo. This was not a conventional professional military force but a police type of formation used to repress tribal uprisings. According to observers, it had a long tradition of "killing, plundering and general mayhem." Because of the absence of trained native officers and an operational code of gangsterism, it degenerated rapidly after independence.

In the Middle East, operational experience has been a record of military defeats. The Turkish army suffered some defeats by

[2] See T. N. Dupuy, "Burma and Its Army: A Contrast in Motivations and Characteristics," *Antioch Review*, Winter, 1960–61, pp. 428–40.

the Europeans in World War I, although it won the major engagement at Gallipoli; the armies of Syria and Iraq were defeated by the French and British mandate in 1920. The Iraqi army was taken over by the British in 1941, and the Iranian army yielded to British and Soviet occupation in the same year. The Arabs were defeated by the Israelis in 1948, and the Egyptian army was defeated again in 1956.

Another type of experience emerged in UN operations in Korea and the Congo. In the Korean conflict Philippine, Thai, and Turkish troops saw extensive combat. In the Congo, Indian, Malayan, and Indonesian armies, with extensive previous experience, performed effectively, and this in turn had an impact on their sense of professional competence. Ethiopian, Nigerian, and Ghanaian troops operated at much lower levels of military effectiveness.[3]

It is an unending question what consequences victory or defeat have on the solidarity and political perspectives of an officer corps. For example, it has been argued that military defeat tends to politicize the military establishment.[4] The case of Ataturk is given as the classic example. However, it should be recalled that Ataturk himself was a successful commander, particularly in repelling the invasion at Gallipoli and in effecting an orderly retreat in Eastern Turkey. Ataturk emerged from World War I as a popular leader with an image of invincibility, and he became the moving figure in ejecting Allied occupation forces from Turkey. Thus, it can be argued that the Turkish example conforms to the contrary proposition that, in new nations, successful military operations

[3] The Moroccan government withdrew its troops as a result of Russian support for its opposition to the admission of Mauritania to the United Nations; Mali withdrew its troops when the Mali Federation broke up; Tunisian troops were withdrawn because of requirements at home; the United Arab Republic and Indonesia withdrew because of disagreement with UN policy in the Congo. Even Sierra Leone sent a small contingent.

[4] On the basis of "a survey of the historical examples of the military effectively encouraging national development," Lucien Pye offers the proposition that "such a relationship is a state of affairs shortly after the country has been defeated or humiliated, but the army has not been seriously damaged and an easy scapegoat exists in the form of discredited civilian elite." Lucien Pye, unpublished paper, December 1961, p. 28.

supply a professional identity, which in turn is the basis for intervention in politics.[5] Nevertheless, it remains hazardous to formulate propositions about the impact of operational experience on the political behavior of an officer corps. Either victories or defeats can serve as a basis of social cohesion, although numerically speaking, in new nations, military success has preceded intervention in domestic politics more frequently than has military defeat. In those nations where the military has had some successful operational experience, especially in suppressing internal insurrections, it has contributed to social cohesion and, in a sense, to the development of an orientation that rises above partisan politics and embodies national ideals. It has made the military more professional, and, all things being equal, successful operational experience leads to further military professionalism, which in turn becomes a firmer basis for intervention in domestic politics.

In planning for their future duties, the armed forces in the new nations have a double outlook. One requirement is to develop conventional forces of the World War II variety. The other requirement is to emphasize internal constabulary functions. Where border security needs are real, and many new nations have an uneasy frontier, or where there is a military threat from a neighboring new nation, a professional response is possible to these conventional threats. Much of the military preparation for conventional warfare, however, is tied to regional and pan-national political aspirations or, alternatively, to the world balance of power. These conceptions of military power may be realistic, but they often have a strong element of national glorification and sheer militarism.

Since the institutions of law and order are fragile in many new nations, the military must be concerned with the alternative function of internal security. To some degree, the same troops and military forces can be utilized for both purposes. Thus, the typical

---

[5] Nasser achieved some personal reputation as a local commander in the 1948 Israeli war. Clearly, the image of the Egyptian army's contribution to forcing the British to relinquish control of the Suez Canal assisted its domestic political role.

army in a new nation organizes elite troops with conventional equipment into units which are deemed especially reliable from a political point of view and which are therefore stationed in or adjacent to the capital city. Their objective is rapid deployment to strategic points in order to insure the security of the political center.

Internal security requirements also lead to the development of special mobile units, including airborne troops, trained to fight insurrectionist forces and to carry out police-type work. The most successful of these internal constabulary operations have been in the Philippines and Malaya. In Burma and Indonesia, operations against insurgent groups, which have been carried out for more than a decade, have been, on the whole, relatively effective. The results of such military operations in India against the Naga and in Iraq against the Kurds have been mixed.

Despite these operational requirements, there is strong pressure within the military profession of the new nations to differentiate themselves from the police. The military, either as a result of the influence of Western forms or because of self-generated heroic ideals, seeks, wherever possible, to withdraw from the continuous task of day-to-day policing and repression of political opposition. When the military is actively involved in internal constabulary operations, it is often more prone to display force than to use force. It seems to operate on the assumption that minor day-to-day resort to force weakens its organizational capacity to intervene successfully with shock tactics and with overpowering impact. This appears to be an application of the military theme of conservation of resources. Paradoxically, such reluctance to be involved in police work increases the ability of the military to intervene in a political crisis period; thereby, the military is frequently free of the stigma of having "pushed people around" and having engaged in "undercover police work."

Thus, the political role of the military is closely linked to the organization and loyalties of the police. The "management of violence" in new nations includes large and extensive police forces, organized on a national basis and on a European gendarmerie model. These police forces are administered generally under a Ministry of the Interior. They have an extensive supply of motor vehicles and portions of their personnel live in military barracks. They are, in effect, auxiliary units to the army but separately organized. In a few countries, where internal disorder is widespread and persistent, these police forces are closely linked to and even under the operational control of the army — for example, in Burma and South Vietnam. In varying forms, new nations also have extensive criminal and secret police organizations.

It is a basic assumption of the democratic model of civilian-military relations that civilian supremacy depends upon a sharp organizational separation between internal and external violence forces. (In the United States, the police have traditionally been a state and local function, in order to facilitate this separation.) In the few countries where it is an instrument of sovereignty, and under civilian democratic political control, the army is completely separated from the police, e.g., in India. However, this arrangement is not widespread in new nations because of the involvement of the army in domestic constabulary duties so as to maintain legitimate authority. Self-conceptions of the military give way to pressures of maintaining internal security. Even in Israel, for example, the army has extensive domestic police duties.

One organizational element that inhibits internal police activities by army units is the fact that in many new nations — especially in former British colonies, but also in countries with as markedly different experiences as Turkey — the military police are not organized into a separate branch of the ground forces with their own channels of command and commanding officers. Instead, they are adjuncts of operational commands (battalions and regiments) and have limited police duties within the military, or in the immediate vicinity of military installations. This contrasts with those circumstances where the military police have their own channels of command, as in some totalitarian countries, and where, as a result, the military police have the dual role of assisting in the control of both the military and the civilian population.[6] Nevertheless, in many new nations, the army has important internal police functions.

When the military becomes the ruling political group and the nation is ruled by a military oligarchy, it must assume direction of the police apparatus just as it must oversee the administration of other agencies of government. Its direct involvement in police administration depends on the loyalty and efficiency of the police and the extent and tactics of the political opposition. With a military takeover of political power, an interpenetration of the army and the police, at the highest levels, tends to develop. There seems little need for extensive purges or reorganization of the police, for the career police officer is prepared to follow the political direction of a military oligarchy.

In nations where an authoritarian one-party system operates to contain the political aspirations of the military, a different system of military-police relations emerges. On a totalitarian model, the police and paramilitary organizations are developed as counterweights to the army. The mass political party makes use of its own secret informers to insure loyalty. In Ghana, for example, special labor units with a paramilitary format, called Toilers' Brigades and organized for economic development, clearly have internal security functions. These Brigades inhibit the potential role of the military in domestic politics. The Convention People's Party, in addition to developing an effective central police force, has a system of secret informers and has made use of party-organized "rowdy" boys for purposes of political coercion. This totalitarian model, in which the armed forces are organizationally

[6] In almost all new nations, the military maintains its own political intelligence activities, partly for purely military operations. These intelligence activities become important resources when the military finds it necessary to become broadly involved with domestic politics. The military can also demonstrate extreme sensitivity to the development of secret police functions by mass political parties. For example, the Burmese army displayed outright hostility to the Bureau of Special Investigation which was organized by U Nu for the purpose of controlling political opponents.

neutralized, can be found in only three countries of the sample of new nations and they — Ghana, Guinea, and Mali — have been clearly influenced by the Soviet model. The dominant pattern, however, is that the armed forces — which in effect means the ground forces — maintain organizational control of the "instruments of coercion."

SKILL STRUCTURE AND CAREER LINES

The exercise of force — actual or threatened — has limited currency as a basis for long-term domestic political power. If the military is able to utilize its organizational power in domestic politics, it is because it has appropriate political leadership skills. Thus, it is necessary to consider the second hypothesis: While there has been a trend toward increased transferability of the professional officers' skill to domestic political activity, the military profession in new nations has important limitations in producing those leadership skills in bargaining and political communications that are required for sustained political leadership.

There is considerable evidence to indicate that, since the middle of the nineteenth century, the transferability of skill from military to civilian roles has grown, as military technology became more complex and as military command came to require elements of persuasion and co-ordination. Nevertheless, this hypothesis is designed to throw light on the difficulties that the typical military oligarchy encounters when it assumes direct political power.

Of course, there are important variations in political skill and involvement among officers. First, within an army, there are certain career and professional experiences which are more likely to increase political competence. Only a minority of the officers may have had such experience. Second, among different armies, the political capacities of a military junta are likely to be deeply conditioned by the attitudes and behavior of its top leader. He may be able to transmit a strong sense of political reality to his immediate followers and to impress on them their political limitations and the need for sharing power with other groups. Third, bright and ambitious officers can become interested in politics because they are sought out and cultivated by political leaders. But these variations should not obscure the underlying skill patterns to be found in the military profession.

One way to analyze the skill structure of the military – of old nations and new – is in terms of its internal division of labor; namely, the heroic leader, the military manager, and the military technologist.[7] The heroic leader embodies traditional themes of martial spirit and personal valor. By contrast, the military manager reflects the growth of the organizational and pragmatic dimensions of warmaking. He is the professional with effective links to civilian society, but he is still concerned with the calculus required for the management of violence. Finally, the military technologist is concerned with incorporating scientific and technological developments of civilian society into the military. Any military establishment requires a balance of the three roles of heroic leader, military manager, and military technologist – a balance which gives greater emphasis to the military manager at the higher level of authority and hierarchy. It is the increase in number and importance of military managers that produces the greater capacity in the profession for involvement in domestic politics.

In new nations, because the infantry unit is the prototype, a significant proportion of the officer's career is involved in training and leading small unit commands. The officer is trained as a commander, which requires a combination of heroic leadership and military management. The typical officer comes to realize that the desired qualities of military management are those of initiative, improvisation, and the taking of responsibility. His professional goals are based on a military calculus, vague and amorphous though that may be. He is not trained in a calculus of profit-making or high-level administration.

In the civilian image, military officers are the personification of Max Weber's ideal bureaucrat. The military is seen as highly

[7] Morris Janowitz, *The Professional Soldier: A Social and Political Portrait* (Glencoe, Ill.: Free Press, 1960), pp. 21–37.

ordered, routinized, and having elaborate rules and regulations. In reality, the military is a crisis organization. While officers are trained to be orderly, they must be prepared to act and respond to the immediate environment. The skill structure of the military profession in new nations means that it is an organization prepared to mobilize its resources in a crisis and especially to challenge tradition.

Engineering and the need to adjust to technological innovations are important day-to-day professional concerns. Most officers must develop some sensitivity to logistics — the procedures for managing the movement of men and matériel. At any given time, most officers are not in command of troops. They are likely to be carrying out administrative duties either within the military establishment or in support installations. This is the case in most armies, including those of the new nations. In the new nations, the typical officer with five to ten years of experience can be useful in managing a particular industrial plant, engineering works, or the like. The transferability of his skill is to middle-level civilian administration.

In general, military experience which emphasizes a simple calculus of violence is not directly transferable to large-scale organizational planning or management. There is no evidence that armies of new nations have a high proportion of staff officers. One reason is that central staff military planning is limited in most of these armies. Only in those countries with extensive foreign aid programs does military planning become meaningful. The absence of extensive staff planning limits officers' experience in high ministerial responsibility, strategic planning, or innovation — either organizational, economic, or political. Only in very large military establishments do officers get the kind of staff experience that prepares them for the highest administrative posts in government.

The difference between military management and political leadership skill is also marked. Political leaders are men who specialize in verbal skills and in mass appeals. In contrast to military officers, they are men who are socialized early into the technique and process of negotiation and bargaining. In particular, the military profession operates in an organizational environment that has limited contact with outside clients, and this, in turn, decreases the transferability of skill from a military to a political career. It is true, however, that as the military develops a more complex technology and the nature of authority changes from domination to group consensus, many of the "human relations" skills of military leadership — concern for morale and internal communications — lead to greater transferability of skill to the civilian political arena. Because of the relatively simple format of the armed forces of the new nations, except for the air forces, and because of the limited sophistication of the enlisted troops, personnel management and authority relations remain relatively old-fashioned and authoritarian and change only slowly.

To point out these deficiencies of political skills is not to overlook the potentialities and assets for developing political orientations. The military profession has a strong sense of public service and this is reinforced by its concept of heroic leadership. Moreover, the military, by its system of recruitment, training, and rotation of personnel to various parts of the nation-state, develops a strong national ethos. Despite its technology, the military is basically not an engineering organization, for it seeks to combine traditional national heroic values with scientific management. In a sense, it is a bridge with the past. Its heroic leaders are concerned with drawing upon cultural traditions, real or imagined, and even with redefining previous military experiences which were not necessarily victorious or heroic.

Different cultural values and attitudes toward authority influence the capacity of a new nation to develop a social structure appropriate to modern technology and economic development.[8] Undoubtedly, a comparative analysis of the military in new nations must confront the different cultural residues of Islam, Hin-

[8] See Lloyd A. Fallers, "Equality, Modernity and Democracy in the New States," Clifford Geertz (ed.), *Old Societies and New Nations* (New York: Free Press of Glencoe, 1963), pp. 158–219.

duism, and the varied ethnic value systems of Sub-Sahara Africa. For example, it can be argued that the values of Islam as implanted in Arab culture are less compatible with modern military authority requirements than are those of Hindu religion and culture. But in general, armies and their ambitious officer cadres are focal points for overcoming barriers to modernization inherent in traditional values based on religion. Either by selection or by training, emerging military officers are generally without strong religious concerns. This is markedly different from the devout overtones of the military establishment in Western countries, where religion, particularly high social-status religion, supplied an element of professional identity and a bridge to aristocratic and, subsequently, to other ruling elites.

Yet it must be repeated that those professional perspectives which press for modernization go hand in hand with almost mystical notions of nation, ethnic group, and polity. The military officer is concerned with maintaining order and with organizing a force that can impose order on an unpredictable environment. His organizing principle is not that of refined scientific humanism but rather of virulent nationalism and crude collective identification. In a context of rapid social change and weak sources of governmental legitimacy, the military constitutes more than a group of professional specialists. As compared with business entrepreneurs and even with the civil service, its personnel become fused into an active political ingredient, because they reflect and incorporate, dramatically and visibly, national aspirations. As new nations strive to establish governments that will be considered legitimate by the population at large, the military clearly constitutes a reservoir of legitimate authority.

All officers do not follow the same career lines, although each military establishment has a conception of the ideal typical professional career. Unique and specialized career opportunities, however, help to develop a small nucleus of officers who are more politically oriented than their typical colleagues. Professional skill in administration, including military management, can be defined as the proficiency employed in adapting available resources to relatively predetermined goals. By contrast, the skill of the political leader — in any setting — must involve shaping new goals as well as mobilizing new resources. In this sense, the military bureaucracy, like any other bureaucracy, has its own political leaders. These political leaders are not only concerned with internal management but also serve to relate the military to external elites and to the variety of publics with whom it must deal. The select military leaders have more of the symbolic negotiating and bargaining skills appropriate for domestic politics.

In new nations, these highly politicized cadres are to be found not only at the highest ranks but also scattered throughout the military hierarchy. In fact, the officers at the very top, especially in ex-colonial armies, are likely to be narrowly professional as a result of their having served under colonial administrations. One observer has sought to identify the rank of colonel as the crucial point at which these political types emerge.[9] Instead of selecting any specific rank as the point at which political capacities emerge, it is more useful to examine the specialized career experiences which produce, or at least stimulate, the development of these political men.

For this purpose it is possible to distinguish types of military careers, i.e., prescribed versus adaptive careers.[10] By the prescribed career, we mean the career of the officer who has followed the idealized pattern. More particularly, he has attended higher staff schools, he has had proper balance of command and staff assignments, and he has avoided becoming overspecialized.[11] By contrast, there are officers whose careers could best be described as adaptive. These officers had the essential elements of the pre-

[9] Manfred Halpern, "Middle Eastern Armies and the New Middle Class," in Johnson, *op. cit.*, p. 312.

[10] Janowitz, *The Professional Soldier*, pp. 168 ff.

[11] A variant of the prescribed career is the routine career. Routine careers characterize those officers who have followed the rules of the game but who, at crucial points in their careers, were not given the opportunity to attend higher command schools but instead developed some technical specialized skill.

scribed career, but, for their time, they had additional and unusual experiences.

In applying these categories to the American military elite of World War II and the post–World War II period, it was discovered that the adaptive career was linked to strong personal motivation which led officers to associate themselves with experimental weapons. Often they were officers who, early in their careers, had unique educational or political-military assignments. Although such assignments were thought to be barriers to a successful career, in the end they helped these officers to enter the military elite because they taught negotiative and innovative skills. Thus, from a sample of 475 high-ranking American officers of the World War II period, 87 were identified as prime movers by fellow professionals and informed observers. More than half of this elite nucleus had had adaptive careers, demonstrating the widespread extent to which entrance into the top echelons of the U.S. military involved such innovating experiences with strong overtones of political-military matters. These officers were concerned not only with technical management of the military but with relating the military to the broader society and to the role of violence in the conduct of foreign affairs.

This same frame of reference helps to explain the political behavior of German generals and the opposition of some to Hitler as expressed by their involvement in the *Putsch* of July, 1944.[12] Social composition was a factor, but not a powerful factor, in fashioning political attitudes. Among a sample of top-ranking officers, there was a tendency for the anti-Nazis — as compared with the "praetorians," those who supported Hitler — to be more upper class or upper-middle class in social origin and to come from Prussian backgrounds. But the real clue to political orientation can be discerned when the adaptive-career officers are compared with those who had followed the typical (prescribed) careers. The typical officer who followed a prescribed career was

[12] Kurt Lang, unpublished paper, 1962.

more likely to be neutral and uninvolved in the struggle. It was among the officers who had adaptive careers that there was either a pro- or anti-Nazi orientation. These were the officers who were connected with new weapons, who rose relatively rapidly, and who had assignments of a political-military nature. To a considerable extent, differences between the anti-Nazis and the pro-Nazis hinged on their network of civilian contacts, their travel abroad, and their educational experiences.

On the basis of observations of informants and the analysis of biographical records, the same career types which produce politically oriented officers are to be found in the new nations. In such countries as Thailand, with a long tradition of military involvement in domestic politics, career specialization becomes institutionalized. The Thai military recognizes a prescribed career mainly concerned with technical and internal professional matters. Officers who show an inclination toward broader political-military activities are selected and specialized for these tasks. In some colonial armies, men entered the military with clear personal political ambitions which, in some cases, had been thwarted in other career settings. Such officers are often sought out by civilian political leaders. In armies formed by national liberation movements, men with deep political involvements formed the original military cadre and continue their political interests as officers. But career experiences are just as crucial in fashioning and developing these adaptive and politically involved officers.

These officers strive for the direct exercise of power and are likely to be found in central command posts. Experience at staff college and exposure to intellectual and political discussions which make up so much of the curriculum of these institutions in the new nations are, together, important sensitizing experiences.

Of the eleven officers in the organizing group of the Egypt Free Officers in 1949, eight were members of the same class in the Military Academy in 1936–39. This class is called the first class, since social restrictions on entrance were removed in that year. Later, most of this group together attended the Staff and Command College during the period 1945–48.[13] Service abroad as an officer in training, or a special political-military assignment, also contributes to this type of career. As in industrialized nations, politically oriented officers are associated with new weapons. In new nations, this means the airborne and paratroop commands (for example, the coup d'état leaders in Laos [successful] and South Vietnam [unsuccessful]). Friendship patterns are important in recruiting and maintaining these nuclei.

Although the concept "marginal man" is ambiguous, it is applicable to these adaptive types. These military leaders are highly Westernized and at the same time strongly nationalistic, with an admixture of traditional themes. Often they display a strange combination of a pragmatic and an ideological orientation. A typical case is that of Lieutenant Colonel Uong Van Dong, who at the age of thirty-two held his last post as director of the Army Staff College of the South Vietnamese army and who had enjoyed the confidence of President Diem himself. He was a professional career officer who attended the French Army Staff College in Paris and spent a year at the United States Army Command and General Staff School in Fort Leavenworth, Kansas. His broad interests led him to acquire training in mathematics and fluency in both French and English. His desire for military and political innovation resulted in exile to Cambodia, after he participated with the battalion of paratroopers who sought to overthrow the Vietnamese government. He was an officer with articulate political beliefs who was vocal about the corruption of civilian politicians. He did not find any incompatibility in his desire for proper government and his resistance to "political control" of the military.

In new nations, because of rapid social change and the speed with which the military have expanded, such officers are able to express their political interests at a much younger age — often in their forties, and in some cases, in their late thirties. In some cases, these adaptive officers must push aside older, more con-

[13] P. J. Vatikiotis, *The Egyptian Army in Politics* (Bloomington: University of Indiana Press, 1961).

servative, and more traditional career-oriented men. In other cases, the pressure of a crisis throws them into key command positions. When the social origins and educational backgrounds of these officers are examined, one sees some sociological basis for their greater political involvement as compared with officers of industrialized nations. Nevertheless, it is the very small minority of adaptive types who supply the politically oriented leadership. Because of the structure of command, these men have influence disproportionate to their number. After they assume power, these men must confront the fact that an officer corps – albeit a politically active corps – and not a political party, is seeking to rule a nation.

SOCIAL RECRUITMENT AND EDUCATION

In the comparative analysis of the military, the next step is to examine patterns of social recruitment, especially to determine whether and how they influence political behavior. It is hazardous, however, to compare the social recruitment of military groups in the new nations with their counterparts in Western nation-states. American sociologists are prepared to engage in comparative analysis of social stratification by applying those categories which they have found appropriate to the social structure of the United States to other countries. When a single and uniform set of categories is applied even to the comparison of England, France, and the United States, let alone to a range of new nations, the result is to oversimplify variations in social history. Nevertheless, there is something to be learned from such comparative analysis, if only to highlight gross differences in social recruitment when they emerge.

Thus, the available evidence strongly supports the third proposition: in new nations, the military is recruited from middle- and lower-middle-class groups. In comparison with the model of Western European professional armies, there is a marked absence of domination by feudal aristocratic and upper-class personnel who are gradually displaced in the nineteenth century by middle-class groups, as the technology of warfare developed.[14] This is an almost obvious finding, since feudalism in North Africa and the Middle East as well as in South Asia and Southeast Asia, did not have those social institutions, in particular a system of land inheritance, which supported an aristocratic pattern of involvement in the military. In Sub-Sahara Africa, it is almost impossible to speak of a feudal tradition, except in Ethiopia. As a result, the proposition applies to the various types of armies in the new nations: the traditionally independent, the ex-colonial, the national liberation, and, of course, the post-liberation formations.

This proposition about social recruitment calls for precise quantitative data. But even in the absence of comprehensive statistical material, the available documentation is rather extensive. These officer corps are relatively small in size, and their social recruitment is amenable to direct observation by social scientists concerned with the study of new nations.

The exceptions to the proposition occur mainly in the Middle East. In fact, only two of the sample of fifty-three nation-states — Pakistan and, to a lesser degree, Egypt — could be said to have a significant number of officers recruited from aristocratic or landed-gentry groups at the time of national independence. Even in these countries, internal politics and the pressures toward professional recruitment have either eliminated or strongly diluted these upper-class elements. In Iraq and Jordan, there was a social equivalent in the presence of tribal chiefs and their kinsmen among the officer group, while there was a significant element of landlords and their sons in the army of Iran.

In addition to the absence of Western-type feudal institutions which fused aristocratic groups with the military, three more specific historical factors help to account for the social origins of the military of the new nations. First, in the Ottoman Empire, it was a long-standing practice of the ruling elites to recruit a bureaucratic class, most often from lower social groups, to staff the military. These officers had primary attachments to the state.

[14] Karl Demeter, *Das deutsche Herr and seine Offiziere* (Berlin: Verlag von Reimar Hobbing, 1935). Janowitz, *op. cit.*, p. 94.

Thus, the colonial powers did not encounter an aristocratic tradition when the dismembered portions of the Ottoman Empire came under Western domination. Likewise, Turkey is a striking example of a traditionally independent nation which did not have to accommodate itself to a strong aristocratic element as it undertook the modernization of its military establishment. As early as the nineteenth century, the army was more representative than other central professional groups, e.g., the bureaucracy and the clergy. In varying degrees, others of the non-colonial sovereign nations gradually divested themselves of their aristocratic officer class as they sought to modernize. In Thailand, by the turn of the century, the military was developing bureaucratic recruitment procedures which drew lower-status personnel from throughout the kingdom. Even in Ethiopia, where outstanding military ability had always been a major means of social mobility into the upper status group, the development of a professional standing army after World War II eliminated the predominance of established feudal lords in the military hierarchy.[15]

Second, the colonial powers tended to weaken the position of aristocratic groups, especially in Southeast Asia. They disbanded the existing armed forces and recruited new and more loyal cadres which did not include such aristocratic elements. If aristocratic elements were recruited into the military, it was because the colonial powers believed that they would fit into their "divide and rule" tactics. In Pakistan, sons of leading families from the northern hill country were recruited into regiments of the Indian army, which later became the core of the Pakistani army at the time of partition. These tribal groups were considered loyal to the British government, if only because of their opposition to Hindu political movements and ethnic groups. In nineteenth-

[15] As so often happens in a nation in which social change is inhibited, transformations can be most dramatic and precipitous. After World War II, the Emperor of Ethiopia decided to expand his elite Imperial Bodyguard. For this purpose he used three successive cadet groups, chosen not because of kinship with noble families, but on the basis of their outstanding performance in secondary schools. One result was that these young middle-class officers became actively involved in a coup d'état against the Emperor.

century Egypt, the upper-status groups who staffed the officer corps were heavily weighted with alien elements — Turks, Kurds, and Albanians — who were a kind of foreign elite, rather than a landed aristocracy. Under the British mandate, Egyptians of aristocratic background were concentrated in a number of elite cavalry units patterned after British high-status regiment. They were part of the system of indirect rule that supported the pashas, and, in fact, these cavalry units were one locus of opposition to the Nasser nationalist movement. Self-selection also operated. Under colonial rule, the low status of the military profession, plus alternative opportunities of civilian education abroad and the possibility of a civil service career, meant that most sons of established families were uninterested in a military appointment.

In recruiting for the military, the colonial powers (Great Britain, France, and the Netherlands) developed a strong ethnic imbalance in order to fashion what they believed to be a politically reliable organization. At first, they recruited enlisted personnel and later officers from tribal groups remote from the central capital, from minority groups, and especially from groups with limited independence aspirations. Frequently these groups came from economically less developed areas and they were therefore attracted by the opportunities in the army.[16] There was also a mysti-

[16] This pattern or recruiting remote or minority groups for military service applies to Morocco, where the French recruited mainly from the Berber-speaking mountain tribes in a country with Arab language and tradition; Syria, where the French relied heavily on linguistic and religious minorities; Indonesia, where the Dutch made use of Christians from the remote eastern islands, especially North Celebes and Ambon; India, where the British recruited heavily from the remote Sikhs; Pakistan, where recruitment was from rural tribes, especially Punjabi and Pathans; Sudan, where there was a strong imbalance of northern Arab officers; Nigeria, where there was strong representation of remote northern Moslem tribes, e.g., Benue and Ilorin; Sierra Leone, where there was overrepresentation from the Mende; Ghana, where recruitment was from the northern tribes which until 1961 supplied 80 per cent of the NCO's; Uganda, where the Acholi predominate at the expense of the Baganda; Kenya, where recruitment was mainly from Kamba and Kalenjin; Northern Rhodesia, where it was heavily from Barotseland and eastern provinces. In Ethiopia, army officers were recruited mainly from the Ahamr people, the ethnic group of the Emperor and the dominant political group. A comparable situation developed in the top leadership of the South Korean army. Under U.S. sponsorship, there was a strong tendency

cal or folkloric element in some of these recruitment policies. Colonial powers believed that men recruited from more primitive areas were better fighters and less contaminated by the corruption of urbanism and Western patterns. Certain of these groups did have strong military traditions, but their political reliability was a crucial factor.

Third, new-nation armies which were organized or extensively modified by the struggle for national liberation are almost completely middle class and lower-middle class, without aristocratic elements. The nationalist movements may have attracted a few prominent older elite families, but, on the whole, nationalist movements and their military formations did not appeal to the aristocratic groups. In Burma, and to some extent in Indonesia, the national armies during World War II recruited widely from university students who had never considered a military career and who were caught up in the struggle for national liberation. While many of these university students returned to their studies, some remained to make the military their career. Men of modest social background and without extensive formal education also became career officers after liberation because of their achievements in guerrilla operations. In the Philippines, Indonesia, Burma, Israel, Morocco, and, more recently, in Algeria, they have been dispersed into the regularly recruited and traditionally trained officer corps.[17]

for Christian officers to rise to prominent positions, and these officers often spoke English; after the coup d'état of 1961, Korean-speaking Buddhists emerged in full force.

[17] A modern military establishment — in a new nation or an old — has certain organizational features which result in the recruitment of its personnel from more representative and humbler social origins than other professions. Despite the material rewards that are offered, life in the military involves many arduous tasks and much physical discomfort. The military attracts recruits from aspiring social groups who are prepared to expose themselves to these discomforts because it does supply an avenue of social mobility. The military also tends to attract the ambitious who recognize that career success in the military is less likely to be affected by their humble social origins than in other professions. In the ethos of the profession, as inherited from Western professional contacts, social background is de-emphasized once a man has been accepted into military service. The military has a combat ideology and is preparing for war — real or imaginary. As a result, it tends

After independence, the pattern of social recruitment in all types of armies tends to converge. The emphasis is on nationwide selection based on educational achievements and other types of selection tests. In the ex-colonial armies, the trend is to reduce dependence on special ethnic groups used by the metropolitan powers. A typical arrangement is that instituted in Nigeria, where the regional recruitment of the military is a delicate political issue. The practice since independence has been to recruit 50 per cent of all recruits from the North and 25 per cent from each of the eastern and western regions. In turn, within the northern region, a provincial allocation is followed to insure representation from the "Far North."

One is struck by the effort to develop a civil-service type of recruitment, with some measure of scientific and unbiased selection, from a wide base of social groups.[18] Pressure for universalistic bases of recruitment comes from foreign advisers employed to train new officer cadres and from older officers who want to develop a self-perpetuating system. Likewise, political leaders seeking to maintain civilian supremacy — either by the weight of Western traditions or by one-party political supremacy — also seem to prefer recruitment of the military on a technical basis. Thus in Ghana, for example, despite the one-party system of rule, no explicit criteria of political loyalty or political screening had — as of 1962 — been introduced.[19]

No civil-service type of recruitment system is free from personal pressure and influence. In new nations, the same pressures are at work that give an advantage to families of influence and political connections. Moreover, even in the highly professional armies of industrialized nations that employ universalistic standards of

to stress the personal worth of the individual man and to ignore his social background.

[18] William Gutteridge, *Armed Forces in New States* (London: Oxford University Press, 1962), p. 13.

[19] Vatikiotis claims that, under the Nasser regime, "in recruiting cadets, Egyptian authorities have continued to discriminate against members of the old aristocracy in favor of small town and village middle-class elements. But they have continued to have an unwritten rule of favoring sons of career officers." *Op. cit.*, p. 232.

recruitment, sons of officers have many advantages. These advantages, particularly in the form of special preparatory schools for sons of officers, are already to be found in some new nations.

To document the absence of a feudal tradition and to point to the broad and broadening base of recruitment is not to assert that there are no special social characteristics of the military.[20] The essential question is how the social profile of the military and its elite members differs from that of other professional and elite groups. There are two selective factors at work. First, there is a disproportionate geographic recruitment of rural and small-town sons, many of whose fathers are small landholders. Of course, it is true that since the new nations are overwhelmingly rural, most elite are recruited from these areas. But the overrepresentation is even greater for the military. Second, there is an occupational inheritance factor — a concentration of sons whose fathers have served in the government, either in the military, in minor civil service posts, or as teachers. Their sons have had the model of success in bureaucratic rather than in free professions. At times, both factors operate in conjunction. Officer recruits are sons of officials and schoolteachers who served in rural areas remote from the major capitals of their countries. William Gutteridge uses the case of Ghana to summarize the question of social recruitment: "An army officer at present is more likely to be the son of a peasant cocoa farmer or a post office official than of a professional man who will probably have educated his son for the bar or the civil service or a similar occupation of established prestige."[21]

What relevance have these findings about the social origins of the military profession to an understanding of its political be-

[20] Only Lucien Pye claims that, for his country, Burma, the top military officers are very much like the top political leaders. Because of the special circumstances in the Burmese army, "The majority of the twenty-three colonels who played key roles in administering the government were at one time either politicians or close associates of politicians. Most of these men were involved in the independence movement and were assigned to an almost random fashion to careers in the army once it became necessary after independence to staff all the institutions of government." Lucien Pye, "The Army in Burmese Politics," in Johnson, op. cit., p. 234.

[21] Op. cit., p. 44.

132 THE INTERNAL ORGANIZATION OF THE MILITARY

havior? There are many steps between the impact of social origin and the political perspectives of a professional group. Especially in the military, the values of early socialization are refashioned by education and career experiences. In shaping the political perspectives of the military, however, social origin seems to be of greater consequence in the new nations than in contemporary Western industrialized countries. Differences in background, such as rural versus urban, are sharper in their social meaning. Moreover, the absence of a feudal tradition is directly relevant for understanding the subsequent impact of both education and professional training. What is so striking is that the combination of hinterland and middle-class social origins plus professional military education does not produce a traditional conservative outlook but, in varying forms, a modernizing and collectivistic orientation.

The feudal tradition of Western Europe was antirational and antitechnological. The history of the military in this area was a history of the struggle of middle-class specialists against aristocratic cavalry officers who loved the style of life of the horseman. In new nations, even under colonialism, the military, as it became a modern profession, was not confronted with this particular social barrier. The professional outlook — the outlook of the military technologist and the military manager — became supreme, particularly in South and Southeast Asia and, more recently, in Sub-Sahara Africa. (The Indian Army emulated many social forms of the older aristocratic tradition, but the officers, both British and Indian, more often thought of themselves as professionals.)[22] In general, in the new nations, the army officer has to strive to establish the image of the heroic fighter and of honor in combat.

It is impossible to make categorical statements about differences

[22] The British Indian army did not have a high component of upper-class officers. From its very origins, through the nineteenth century, the concentration of upper-class and gentry in the British Indian army was much lower than in the British home army. The same was probably true for the French forces, since the rigors of colonial service abroad did not appeal to aristocratic elements. See Peter E. Razzell, "A Sociological History of Officers in the Indian and British Home Armies: 1758–1912," Paper No. 1, Center for Social Organization Studies, University of Chicago, May, 1962.

in attitude toward politics in armies with feudal social origins and aristocratic traditions as compared with middle-class–based institutions. To speak of the conservative outlook of the feudal origin and the revolutionary outlook of the middle-class — or to compare the Prussian Junker with the middle-class Bonapartist — is an oversimplification. For the Western military profession, however, feudal tradition operated to inhibit direct intervention by the military in domestic partisan politics. The feudal military aristocrat had a conservative outlook. Yet his conception of politics was that he was above politics. He sought to rely on other elements in the elite for achieving his political ends. In England, this aristocratic outlook led to the development of effective civilian and parliamentary supremacy. In Germany, it led to Prussian-type militarism, since such was the content of conservative politics, and subsequently to the acceptance of National Socialism. As the military in the West became a middle-class profession, one consequence was that the profession was opened to more direct political involvement. This was not simply because of the change in social origin but also because of the revolution in military affairs that required broader political perspectives among professional officers.

By contrast, the absence of such an aristocratic tradition has meant the absence of a historical tradition which would limit the military in its political involvement. The military is a professional and bureaucratic group, and therefore, like other such groups, it is directly involved in administrative politics. To the degree that it considers itself above partisan politics, this notion is rooted in professional ideals and not in aristocratic disdain for political action. Likewise, the absence of an aristocratic social tradition implies that the military has less of a stake in the existing social structure. While its middle-class social origins hardly determine its professional ideology, they do contribute to a bureaucratic and managerial outlook which is congenial to gradual modernization and social change.

The rural, or, more accurately, the hinterland social background, coupled with petty middle-class or bureaucratic occupational origins, contributes to a "fundamentalist" orientation and to a lack of integration with other elites, especially the political elite. Particularly in the Middle East and in North Africa, but also in other new nations, there is a split in values between the hinterland and the metropolitan social fabric. Since the officer class has its roots in the countryside, its ideological orientation is critical of sophisticated upper-class urban values, which it comes to consider as corrupt and even decadent. This anti-urban outlook is strong in professional armies in other parts of the world, and it seems to be reinforced by the professional indoctrination and style of life of the military community. These aspects of the social background of the officer corps seem to have almost contradictory implications. The military is hostile to what it believes are self-indulgent urban values; yet it is oriented to modernization and to technological development. Social background together with their educational experiences operate to make military officers accessible to politics, but at the same time there is a social gulf between them and the cadres of political leaders who are much more attracted to the sophisticated culture of the major capitals.

The social origins of the military must also be related to the motives of those who choose a military career. Given the prevailing emphasis on commercial values and business success in the United States, the selection of a military career is believed to be a weak career choice. By a weak career choice is meant a career decision which does not represent strong ambition, powerful ideals, or a sense of personal self-confidence. Among segments of the civilian public, entry into the military is often considered an effort to avoid the competitive realities of civil society. In the extreme view, the military profession is thought to be a berth for mediocrity. In Western Europe, as in the United States, the same notions prevail but not to the same degree. In the past, those aristocrats and the rural gentry in particular, as well as those select middle-class families with a tradition of military service, who sent their sons into the profession did so not out of public recognition, but because they believed that the military was an appropriate style of life. But with the development of an industrialized society, the military profession has not been able to develop the kind of public prestige it deems worthy of its traditional calling.

In new nations also, the military profession suffers in social esteem. Under colonialism, the prestige of the military was low.[23] Since the end of colonial rule, the prestige of the military as a profession has risen only slightly — much less than might have been expected. The increased importance of the army as a mark of sovereignty, larger budgets, and the broadened internal functions of the military all work to increase prestige. The prestige of the profession is at sharp variance with the reputation of key military figures who come to be acclaimed as national heroes.

Sociologists measure occupational prestige by comparing opinions about the attractiveness of one occupation in contrast to others and by investigating young people's hypothetical interest in entering the profession. In these terms, the prestige of the military, even after independence, remains low. Thus, a study of Ghanaian middle-class schoolboys, based on data collected after independence, revealed that only 5 per cent wanted to enter the profession, and they rated the military as falling toward the middle of the occupational prestige hierarchy.[24]

In the past as in the present, however, the relative occupational prestige of the military is no adequate index to the actual supply of manpower or the range of motives for entering the profession. On the basis of direct empirical research in the United States and corroborative evidence for Western Europe, we can see that the military career, despite its low prestige, represents a strong career choice for at least a sizable minority, and especially for young men from the hinterlands. As a strong career choice, it gives expression to personal ambition for social mobility and to the desire

[23] The prestige of the military appears higher in Pakistan, because of the heritage of martial and traditional values.

[24] Unpublished report by Philip Foster, Committee for the Comparative Study of Education, University of Chicago, 1962.

for collective achievement. Many recruits tend to be young men from humble families who have had secondary education and who are seeking an avenue of social mobility. As is currently the case in Western nation-states, they do not come from elite backgrounds but develop a leadership outlook in their professional training. These young men see the military as representing fundamental and desirable values. They choose the military because it is accessible to men of their social position and regional background. They choose the military because they believe that their social background will not constitute a hindrance to career success. They are expressing their interest in collective goals as opposed to the personal goals of business — again reflecting the clash of values between the hinterlands and the metropolitan centers.

Available evidence, from biographical sources and informant interviews, reveals that the same career motivation is at work in the new nations. For an important minority, the pattern of attracting the ambitious and the "visionary" was already at work in the colonial armies. Thus, such men as Nasser and his comrades entered the army, despite its low prestige, because they believed that in the long run it would supply the opportunity for liberating and modernizing their homeland. For some of these men to choose the low-prestige military career reflected a long-term, realistic outlook rather than an immediate careerist interest. Another indication of these multiple motives of realism, sheer ambition, and desire for group accomplishment is the fact that, under colonial regimes, many entered the military after a period of frustration in other careers, particularly as schoolteachers and lawyers.[25]

Strongly motivated persons were recruited into the officer ranks of armies established in the "struggle for liberation" during World War II. Under such circumstances, recruitment was highly self-selected and involved strong ideological commitments or strong feelings of personal injustice. This was particularly the case in nations occupied by the Japanese, where recruits into the military came directly from secondary schools and universities, under the

[25] Majid Khadduri, "The Role of the Military in Middle Eastern Politics," *American Political Science Review*, June, 1953, p. 517.

assumption that collaboration with the Japanese would result in national independence. When their ambitions were frustrated, these recruits were prepared to embark on guerrilla warfare and other types of independent action.

Since independence, the number of potential recruits, both enlisted and officer, has far exceeded available openings, despite continued relatively low prestige.[26] The very high number of applicants — both officer and enlisted — is a result of the expanded educational system and the limited number of alternative opportunities. Undoubtedly, there is a strong trend toward careerism among the ever increasing number of aspirants. Some of this careerism can be inferred from the fact that one important source of recruitment in the post-liberation armed forces is from graduates of technical and engineering schools who see, in the armed forces, a secure opportunity to practice their specialized skills. But powerful ambition and strong motivation, both for self-advancement and national service, still persist among those who offer themselves to the officer selection boards.

In most new nations, officer education serves to reinforce the proclivities of the officer corps toward involvement in domestic politics. The classic model for professional officer training during the nineteenth century made early recruitment into the profession and education under military auspices desirable and essential requirements. The British Navy took young lads of twelve to fourteen years of age as cadets who would later be developed into officers. The Junkers developed the *Kadettenschule* as a military equivalent of secondary schools, after which officer training in a military academy was indispensable.

In this view, military education, instead of a general university education, was thought to be necessary for infusing loyalty into the officer corps and for the heroic posture required to face the dangers of battle. An important by-product of military education was that the officer corps was isolated from civilian political pres-

[26] William Gutteridge, for example, reports that in Ghana, at the Kumasi Training Center, there were as many as 1,500 applicants for forty openings for enlisted recruits. *Op. cit.*, p. 34.

sures, or at least indoctrinated in accepting the political status quo — whether that were parliamentary control in Great Britain or allegiance to the Prussian king. As the importance of technical training grew, the military sought to establish its own technical and engineering training schools in order to have specialists with the appropriate professional esprit de corps. In the United States, where military professionalism was strongly resisted, the Army and the Navy were able to found their own military training academies. Yet, over the long run, these military academies supply only a small portion of active-duty officers. Among new nations, the more recent the origins of the military, the more civilian is the educational base from which officers are recruited. Officer education is one form of professional education. But the educational content, as contrasted with the professional content, is not very much different from the educational content of other professional groups. The pattern conforms more to the American practice than to the European, or German, form. Only in Turkey, where many military practices date back to German influences, does the army operate secondary school systems and limit entrance into the officer corps to graduates of the military academy. In the new nations generally, military academy training, which takes two or three years, begins after civilian secondary school education. Leading secondary schools often have cadet officer corps. In many countries, recruiting is articulated with university education, in that officer candidates have some university-level training. Technical specialists are recruited after they have completed their civilian technical education. As a result, much of the officer's education exposes him to social and political influences similar to his generation in other professions and contributes to his political interest. Under colonial rule, secondary civilian schooling already meant that students were often exposed to political and nationalist agitation. At the university, political agitation was intense, and this tradition continued after independence.

In some countries, officers receive their basic military education abroad, or are sent abroad for advanced training, which also has the consequence of strengthening political interests in general and fostering concern with social change rather than with fashioning a particular ideology. For example, in Turkey, the contemporary reawakening of political interests among junior officers is a result of the extensive overseas training that some of these officers have had and of the broadening cultural horizons that such training produces.

PROFESSIONAL AND POLITICAL IDEOLOGY

It is not possible to speak of an ideology among military officers in the new nations. Instead, the fourth proposition states that, because of diversity rooted in cultural and historical background, it is possible only to speak of some more or less common ideological themes. These common themes are grounded in the social composition of the officer corps, their education, and their professional experience — more in education than in social composition, and more in professional experience than in education. Nevertheless, these themes make possible the general observation that, while the military of the new nations have ideological orientations common to their counterparts in Western industrialized nations, they display some common and crucial differences. Their nationalism and their "puritanical" outlook are similar to their Western counterparts. Differences center on their greater acceptance of "collectivist" forms of economic enterprise and on their more powerful hostility toward politicians and organized political groups.

First, at the core of these themes is a strong sense of nationalism and national identity, with pervasive overtones of xenophobia. In varying degree this outlook adheres to the military as a profession. Profession and career seem to produce few experiences which work to counter this xenophobia. One consequence of this powerful attitude of national identification is that the military becomes a strong source of anticommunal sentiment. Even under colonial rule, where the communal composition was carefully manipulated, once the officer had entered the military, communal issues were taboo. As the military becomes more representative of the social structure, the code of professional ethics operates to repress tribal and separatist attachments.

A second and widespread element is a strong "puritanical" outlook and an emphasis on anticorruption and antidecadence. This again seems to be a rather universal characteristic of the military profession and reflects, to some degree, the underlying motives of those who select this career. The desire to be strong and unyielding is reinforced by the rigors and routines of daily existence. But the military demands these qualities not only for itself but for society as a whole, and it sets itself up as a standard-bearer of hard work and unflinching dedication.

The military view of morality describes modesty and self-restraint in one's private life as essential for fighting corruption in political and governmental life. Thus, in July, 1962, the military junta in South Korea took action against inefficient and insubordinate governmental officials. Among charges they levied were not only those of black-marketeering activities but also of "keeping concubines." Strong emphasis is placed on a modest style of life, and military leaders are sometimes conspicuous in their nonindulgence in alcohol and tobacco. This asceticism is another source of tension with other elites, especially with new political elites, who use conspicuous consumption as a way to validate their authority and position.

Third, at the root of military ideology is the acceptance of collective public enterprise as a basis for achieving social, political, and economic change. In this respect, the military of new nations differs in degree from older nations, where social origin and training reinforce "conservative" thinking. A scattering of officers in the Middle East have become outright Communists (Communist penetration in Iraq was probably the most extensive).[27] The Indonesian air force, as a young and highly technologically oriented military formation, is strongly leftist. The same

[27] Walter Z. Laqueur, *Communism and Nationalism in the Middle East* (New York: Praeger, 1956).

appears to be the case in Egypt. More typically, however, the desire for governmental intervention is moderate. In the Middle East, this leads to acceptance of socialist symbolism. After the military coup in Syria in 1962, the officer group in control, who could hardly be called radicals, announced their adherence to a "constructive and just socialism."[28] In Southeast Asia, where the military confronts leftist political parties, they do not use socialist symbols, although their specific objectives involve extensive governmental control of the economy. In Sub-Sahara Africa, political trends within the military are only unfolding, but their proclivities for governmental intervention are clear. In general, officers are more interested in organizational forms than in ideological justifications. Such collectivist orientation is stronger among young officers, who also have more pronounced ideological concerns.[29]

Fourth, and perhaps, in the long run, the most pervasive theme, is an "anti-politics" outlook of the military. Interest in politics goes hand in hand with a negative outlook and even hostility to politicians and political groups. It is the politics of wanting to be above politics. In fact it could be said that, if the military of the new nations has an ideology, it is distaste for party politics. Among offcers, there is no glorification of or even respect and understanding for the creative role of the politican and the political process. The accomplishments of civilian politicians are too few to produce respect among the military, and the contacts between them are not sustained enough to engender trust. Instead, the military is suspicious and hostile toward political leaders, particularly in the Middle East. In part, this reflects the oppositional mentality which is so strong among all types of professional leadership groups in the new nations. It is an expression of their resentment of older elites who accumulated profits and privileges in what they believe to have been a weak and ineffective society.

[28] *New York Times*, March 29, 1962.
[29] There is a partial element of truth in the jest among journalists who report on new nations, that generals' revolutions are status quo revolts; colonels' revolts are socialist; while those of majors and captains will be Communist.

Military leaders, because of their image of heroic leadership, distrust the bargaining process in organized party politics. But in the industrialized societies of the West, where civilian supremacy has become institutionalized — in both multiparty and one-party systems — the professional military has at least learned to respect the skills of the political leader.[30] But in the new nations, with some notable exceptions such as India, the military has not had the occasion to develop a sense of respect for the competence and commitment of the politician.

This antipolitical orientation is an expression of the military's technocratic thinking. As soldiers, they tend to believe that any problem is amenable to a direct and simple solution. Leaders are men who can identify the heart of a situation — be it technical, military, or social — and who are prepared to drive through to the desired outcome. As soldiers, they are repulsed by compromise, by indirect solutions, and by the willingness of political leaders to temporize as a way of solving problems. In fact, if military officers succeed in the use of political power, it is because they develop an understanding of the limits of politics and of the complex processes by which human beings are mobilized for political ends.

The ideology of the military has a style as well as a content. In this style, it is difficult to separate the distinctive military elements from some of the intellectual overtones that one finds in many new nations. The military professional tends to be an anti-introspective even when he has intellectual interests. His rhetoric is characterized by a bold assertiveness. Military men regard themselves as doers rather than as thinkers. Despite their strong convictions, there is an element of superficiality in their efforts to develop an ideology. The educational tradition to which these officers have been exposed, both civil and military, has not had the consequence

[30] Thus, for example, when a sample of U.S. military cadets were asked what careers they would like to pursue if they were unable to be officers, one-quarter stated "politics." John P. Lovell, "The Cadet Phase of the Professional Socialization of the West Pointer." (Ph.D. dissertation, University of Wisconsin, 1962), p. 145.

of developing a profound sense of history — either indigenous or foreign. Their educational institutions have not been concerned with developing effective self-criticism; instead, they have been more attuned to developing a sense of identity. Such educational influence supports and strengthens the assertiveness of the military. As a result, the "mentality" of the military officer seems to be a mixture of half-developed but strongly held ideology and a deep sense of pragmatic professionalism.

The ideological themes of the military — in new nations and old — are not grafted onto the profession, but have evolved in the course of the history of the particular army. But compared with other institutional groups in the new nations, the military has a strong sense of realism and detachment. Training in technology and contact with foreign specialists sensitizes military personnel to the relative backwardness of their countries. They are aware of the possibility of change, since they are superficially familiar with the events of colonialism and have more directly experienced recent political changes which produced independence. They understand the importance of force and perhaps exaggerate its relevance for directing social and political change. But because military leaders are strongly nationalistic, and because of their heroic posture, their sense of realism can be easily exaggerated.

Ideology is not the obverse of realism. Elite groups must have a sense of vision and high purpose grounded in some universalistic belief. Particularly in the new nations, with their profound problems of economic and social development, the military's zealous commitment to public service and its asceticism are as important as its sense of realism. Even its "operational" outlook may serve as a partial substitute for a political ideology, to the extent that it encourages an exploration of alternative political forms.

COHESION AND CLEAVAGE

Cohesion — the feeling of group solidarity and the capacity for collective action — is an essential aspect of the military profession's internal organization that conditions its political behavior. The degree of cohesiveness is a function of a wide variety of specific sociological and organizational factors. But, in the simplest terms, the fifth proposition states that armies with high internal cohesion will have greater capacity to intervene in domestic politics. Moreover, once they have embarked on political intervention, cohesive military elites are more able to limit their involvement, if such is their intent, or they are better equipped to follow consistent policies. Lack of cohesion leads to unstable and fragmented involvement and to the likelihood of counter-coups d'état after the seizure of power. Thus, this proposition about internal cohesion is designed to clarify differences among the new nations rather than differences between old and new nations.

One political expression of a cohesive military organization is the decision of the top commander and his immediate subordinates to assume power, as in the case of Pakistan or Burma. The action takes the form of a military command, and the officers corps responds in a unified fashion. But military "takeovers" are often the result of a powerful faction acting without the "legitimate" authority of the top commander, as in Egypt. For such an operation, a high degree of cohesion is still required. While Nasser and his group of collaborators were relatively unknown to the Egyptian public, they had become a cohesive group through common educational experience and years of internal military politics. They commanded the respect and informal loyalty of wide segments of the officer corps.

Empirical analysis of organizational cohesion can be highly precise, when quantitative measures can be collected on sociometric patterns or on attitudes, or even when estimates can be made on the basis of direct observation. The available data, based on informed observer judgments, are relevant for some specific countries but hardly comprehensive enough to permit a systematic testing of the proposition about cohesion. As a result, it is only possible to attest to its plausibility. It is useful, therefore, to set forth the various factors that strengthen or weaken cohesion in a military officer corps.

For example, the effective Turkish experience after World War I was based upon cohesive elements that Ataturk was able to develop that dated back to the original young Turk revolt of 1908.[31] Until its most recent involvement, the Turkish army has maintained effective internal discipline and has been able to act as a solid force. Likewise, the political behavior of the Burmese army has been the result of a highly cohesive military elite which has been exposed to common professional experiences. South Korea and Pakistan are additional examples of cases where organizational cohesion contributed to the military's ability to intervene initially. Internal cohesion can be a factor in the acceptance of civilian supremacy, as in the cases of India, Malaya, and Israel.

The Sudanese military represents the case of a relatively integrated military, but with significant internal cleavages which have complicated its political intervention. One source of cleavage was the ethnic imbalance between northern Arab officers, who dominated the army, and the southern Nilotic minority that finally led to a revolt in 1955. Greater unity emerged from this conflict because of a conscious policy which stressed ethnic heterogeneity and balance. A more persistent source of tension in the Sudanese army is the gap between two age groups of officers. One group, the older, was commissioned and had its formative experiences under the colonial regime, particularly during the expansion period of World War II. The second group, the younger, was rapidly commissioned in the "crash" program of 1952–53, when the nation became independent and required a larger military force. After the military assumed political power, the younger officer group, stationed mainly in the provinces, repeatedly sought to launch counter-coups with radical objectives. Although the older group had to make concessions to these officers, they were able to dominate and direct the nature of the military regime that was created. By contrast, an example of a military establishment with strong cleavages is the Indonesian, where regional loyalties prevent the

[31] In fact, the organizational format of the modern Turkish army had its origins in reforms of the early nineteenth century.

emergence of a unified political force. Other examples of countries where lack of cohesion has weakened political potentials include South Vietnam, Ceylon, Syria, Lebanon, Ethiopia, and the Congo.

Social cohesion rests on primary-group solidarity and on personal loyalties that men develop toward each other. But social cohesion is more than a process of primary-group solidarity. In fact, primary-group solidarity can be so particularistic that it weakens and inhibits the cohesion of an institution and creates organizational cleavages. Social cohesion requires that primary-group solidarity operate to integrate the larger organization. Social cohesion in the military requires effective procedures for assimilating new personnel, meaningful authority and sanction systems, allocation of equitable rewards and promotions, and a sense of organizational purpose.

In the new nations' armies, cohesion and cleavage center as much on organizational and career experiences as on social composition or ethnic and religious background. A pervasive characteristic of the military is that it is a profession which regulates the total life cycle as well as the daily cycle of its members. It is a profession in which place of work and place of residence overlap to produce what has come to be called "total institutional" life. Such institutional existence contributes strongly to a sense of professional identification by removing the individual from counterpressures of the larger community and civilian society. But in the new nations, the military is less a "total institution" than in Western societies. Much of the personnel is stationed in very small units scattered throughout the country rather than in large centralized installations, so that there is extensive daily contact with civilians. The boundaries of the military are less clearly drawn, and, therefore, the distinction between the military and the nonmilitary is not as sharp.

Training and indoctrination are designed to produce a unified value system. Compared with other institutions, the military establishment seems to have a high capacity for amalgamating new recruits and developing a strong sense of cohesion. But the process of assimilation is a continuous one, so that the officer is acutely aware of the career generation to which he belongs. The strong pressures toward social cohesion based upon uniform training and indoctrination are weakened by sharp intergenerational cleavages of younger versus older officers, a source of cleavage with particular political import. Younger officers with less seniority have fewer vested interests in the military system. They are less involved in the social and political status quo and more involved in contemporary political currents, with the result that they are inclined toward a more radical outlook.

The promotion system is designed to deal with this intergenerational cleavage by regulating the flow of officers through the ranks and by holding out to new recruits the promise of a successful and orderly career. Professional procedures contribute to cohesion where they are able to eliminate incompetent officers and where promotion is clearly recognized as resting on merit. However, the promotional systems of the new nations vary to a great degree. In some countries, the concept of an orderly career has not yet developed, since there are no procedures for eliminating unfit officers and no system for orderly retirement. Where rapid economic growth is taking place, as in Israel, early retirement may be possible because officers can be quickly assimilated into civilian posts. Where the possibility exists for a continuous promotion system, there is a reduction of tension between younger and older generations. More typically, in most new nations, rapid expansion of the military means that the officer corps is filled with men of roughly the same age. This introduces serious promotional problems and increases the likelihood of frustration and intrigue in the junior ranks, because of limited opportunities for promotion. Since rotation of assignment is not as well developed as in Western armies, cleavages emerge between those officers and troops assigned to the capital and its environs and those who spend their careers in regional garrisons or in the hinterlands.

Successful operational experience is another basis for cohesion. Again, as long as the military is fashioned after the infantry model, a common set of experiences contributes to organizational cohesion. But with the development, slow though it may be, of naval and air force interservices, rivalry increases and becomes a significant element. Likewise, relations with the police are a basis for cohesion or cleavage. To the degree that the military is able to separate itself from the police function, it has an additional basis of internal solidarity. But to the degree that it must overlap in function and in personnel with day-to-day police activities, cleavages develop between police-oriented and military oriented officers. Finally, cleavage develop between officers who must carry on routine activities of the military and those who are involved in policy and administrative direction.

One area of potential cleavage which seems not to have materialized is the difference between those officers trained in regular warfare and those incorporated from guerrilla units. Ex-guerrilla officers seem to be absorbed into the regular structure. Similarly, there seems to be little resentment against officers because they served as officers during the colonial period. One device for overcoming cleavages can be the retirement or expulsion of groups of officers whose political sympathy is not with the central authority. For example, in 1957, officers trained in eastern Arab countries who might sympathize with Nasser were eased out of the Tunisian armed forces.

There can be no mechanical approach to the analysis of cohesion and cleavage. Thus, for example, there is a point at which multiple sources of diversity supply a new basis for cohesion. If an army has some of its officers trained in and by a foreign nation, one might suppose that this would create an important cleavage. But in the cases of the Thai and Burmese armies, the great variety of foreign sources of assistance have had their specific impacts, none of which has been paramount. The sense of not having relied on any particular foreign establishment, but on contributions from the military profession per se, has become a source of social solidarity.

Military organizations seem particularly vulnerable to rivalries generated by the clash of personalities, which in turn may develop into political rivalries. There is a difference between the sense of cohesion within an officer corps as a whole and the social solidarity of its elite members. Men of strong ambition recognize that the top leadership post can be occupied by only one man and that opportunities for even sub-leadership are limited. As a result, cliques develop that represent no more than personal followings and personal ambitions but that subsequently assume political significance.

Finally, what does the officer's sense of professional cohesion do to his communal ties and his familial contacts? To what extent are military officers different from other bureaucratic officials or professionals in severing relations with their kinsmen? The ability of the military to act as an effective political force depends upon the development of universal perspectives unencumbered by familial and territorial attachments.

Sociological and anthropological literature on the social structure of new nations emphasizes the importance and pervasive character of familial and kinship connections. It is argued that new nations are societies in which these attachments are strong and persistent, as compared with the social fabric of industrialized nations. The strength of these ties is rooted in cultural values and in familial authority. It is generally presumed that modernization requires that kinship ties be weakened, since they are barriers to effective large-scale organization. But cultural values and patterns of familial authority operate in new nations to maintain kinship ties in the face of modernization. The very fact that the emerging middle class is so relatively small contributes to the persistence and importance of kinship relations. Furthermore, most new occupational specialties become concentrated in the few major urban centers of a new nation and thereby form an ecological base which contributes to the reinforcement of kinship ties.

In some respect, the military is no different from other professions in the new nations in its kinship ties. Like other professional groups, the military recruits persons whose kinship ties are particularly strong, because they are rooted in the rural areas of their birth. Similarly, military officers try to maintain contact with their relatives in other occupational and professional groups which make up the small middle class. It can be argued, however, that the military is more likely than other professional groups to have its members' kinship ties loosened and their sociometric ties more rooted within the organization. Professional education and military assignments and the institutional life in military strain and weaken kinship ties. Most important is the system of authority and ethics that emphasizes professional loyalty at the expense of familial traditions. This is particularly true among officers who rise into positions of high authority or who are involved in the innovative processes of the military.

As the military assumes broader political roles, its members are, at times, forced into conflict with these specific attachments to family groups. A good example of this is the clash of interests generated about land reform, where the broadening scope of land reform may conflict more and more with the interests of relatives. Nevertheless, these conflicts tend to be resolved in terms of the political necessities which confront the military profession.

3. ARMY AND SOCIETY

SOCIAL AND ECONOMIC FUNCTIONS

There is still another aspect of a military establishment in a new nation that conditions its political behavior. Even where armies are limited in their political role, they have economic and social functions which influence political change. It is by no means easy to evaluate, on a comparative basis, the consequences that these economic and social activities have for political change and their effect on the military.

The military accumulates a considerable amount of material and technological resources. For most new nations, the cost of an armed force represents a major expenditure, military assistance notwithstanding (see Table 2 in chap. I). Basically, it is impossible to assess the economic consequences of military activities without raising the question of the alternative use which a new nation might make of these resources. But narrow questions can be explored. What are the direct and indirect contributions to economic development of military expenditures? Two classes of activities are primarily involved: first, the military serves as a training ground for technical and administrative skills; and second, the military manages economic enterprises to meet its own requirements or for the needs of civilian society.

Technical training started as a result of expanded military operations during World War II. During World War II, military training was an important source of technical assistance to underdeveloped countries, where colonial armies mobilized native troops. The result in those countries was to expose more manpower to technical training and organizational discipline. From a relative point of view, this was particularly the case in Sub-Sahara Africa, where it is estimated that nearly one-half million Africans were mobilized during World War II.[1] Most were given some rudimentary training appropriate for modernization, and a minority received technical training dealing with motor vehicle maintenance, sanitation, and simple technical skills.

After World War II, mobilization was cut back sharply in these ex-colonial powers. As the relative importance of technical training in the military decreased, civilian government and private training schemes developed. Moreover, the military is a heavy consumer of its own trained personnel, and the numbers produced are limited even in countries with extensive military establishments. Thus, for example, the Pakistani army, which has a special school for apprentices, was turning out only 250 technicians annually during the late 1950's.[2] Therefore, the contribution of the military to technical training, while important, should not be exaggerated.

In a number of countries — Burma is a pertinent example — the armed forces maintain their own economic enterprises, which range from manufacturing plants to department stores. In Burma, the Defense Service Institute, which was mainly concerned with supplies to the military establishment, was expanded in 1961 to include the Burma Economic Development Corporation. Through this device, the army controls commercial concerns involved in

[1] James Coleman, in John J. Johnson, *The Role of the Military in Underdeveloped Countries* (Princeton, N.J.: Princeton University Press, 1962), p. 396. It is estimated that in the Gold Coast some 65,000 to 70,000 men were recruited and an even larger number in Nigeria. William Gutteridge, *Armed Forces in New States* (London: Oxford University Press, Institute of Race Relations, 1962), p. 28.

[2] "The Pakistan Army," *Asian Review*, January, 1959, pp. 39–44.

steel production, pharmaceuticals, cement, and shipping. Generally, such economic enterprises are designed to assist the army in performing its military functions and they do not necessarily contribute to economic growth. The military often expands into economic development activities, however, particularly in land reclamation work.

As a result, the military develops a pool of trained managers who are available for public and private industries. These are either retired officers or officers who have been assigned to governmentalized industries. In Indonesia, Israel, and Egypt, for example, former army officers are to be found in key managerial posts of governmental industries.[8] Alternative ways of training such managers are available, and in some new nations, e.g., Egypt, national schools of economic administration are being developed.

The economic function of the military includes its contribution to developing public works, roads, and engineering projects. Such projects can be found throughout most new nations, but, with some notable exceptions, their importance is more symbolic than economic. The armed forces have special capacities to assist in relief and economic rehabilitation after major national disasters, floods, earthquakes, etc. As was the case when the western frontier of the United States was developed, the military seems to be used as a cutting instrument to undertake new, unconventional, and dramatic projects rather than developments in depth. Where extensive public works programs are undertaken, they are likely to be in the hands of civilian enterprises, either private, governmental, or foreign.

The ability of the military to act as a political coalition partner often depends upon the extent of its own economic base. The more economic resources it has at its command, the greater is its scope for domestic politics. In turn, the scope of its economic enterprises seems to expand with the broadening of its political involvement. But the economic functions of the military change when the

---

[8] In the case of Indonesia, some of these officers received their rudimentary training in management at the Command and General Staff School, Fort Leavenworth, Kansas.

military assumes direct political power. The army is called upon to give direction to an economic system when it becomes either a caretaker government or the ruling military oligarchy. The consequences for economic development under these forms of political rule are by no means clear-cut. In the initial stages, the military has important organizational assets. Its public-service tradition makes possible a surveillance of the economic sector in the name of a strong, but not necessarily effective, anticorruption drive. The military is able to contribute to the more orderly management of transportation, sanitation, and related activities. Because its orientation is not profoundly religious, it presses for the elimination of religious conventions which thwart economic development. When economic management involves the direction of public corporations for handling specific commodities, military regimes have shown vigor and competency. For example, the Sudanese military was effective in stabilizing the production, allocation, and sales of cotton, and the Burmese army intervened in rice and meat distribution. In contrast, the Indonesian army has not been able to overcome the extensive corruption and mismanagement of the commodity market which developed and persisted under civilian political government.

The more fundamental issue, however, is the strategic contribution of the military to management of economic development, either in specific sectors in which they concentrate their efforts or in the over-all rate of economic growth. While the results on either score are mixed, the outcome indicates basic limitations of the military in supplying economic leadership to a new nation. To intervene decisively on a sustained basis in a limited sector may drain its personnel resources, while to supply ministerial direction to economic regulatory agencies presents the military with problems for which it has inadequate training and skills and no adequate goals.

Assumption of direct political power means that the military must become involved in management of agricultural production and land reform for a combination of economic and political reasons. The military approach to land reform is gradualist, even in a country like Egypt where socialist goals are explicit. Land reform involves the breakup of the very largest estates and their redistribution to landless peasants. While these land reform programs have immediate political appeal, they do not bring about an increase in agricultural production. The military also continues reclamation of new lands, mass irrigation projects, and the so-called community development schemes that are designed to improve agricultural technology and social welfare services in rural areas.

Whatever moderate success in the agricultural sector has been achieved by military governments in countries with food deficits is lost to the ever increasing population base. Therefore, after some delay, military leaders of both Pakistan and Egypt have explicitly accepted family planning and birth control as national policy. The modernism of the military predisposes it to such programs, and its organizational skills are well adapted to develop them.

In Indonesia, the army's efforts in agriculture failed because of organization inertia and the shortage of appropriate personnel.[4] After independence, large colonial agricultural estates were nationalized rather than broken up into small holdings. The army was crucial in preventing left-wing groups from assuming control of these estates, and it developed extensive aspirations for managing them. But military participation in their management has been very limited and ineffective. Instead, civilian bureaucrats are key figures at the regional and local levels.

As measured by over-all economic development, the experience of military regimes is hardly impressive. During the first period of military government in Burma, economic development was not markedly increased, although there was general improvement in government administration. The Pakistani military government has shown a great deal of initiative in economic management, and

[4] J. S. C. Mackie, "Indonesia's Government Estates and Their Masters," *Pacific Affairs*, Winter, 1961–62, pp. 337–60.

the central ministries are run by civilian experts and professionals who have been given considerable autonomy. Yet, partly because of the heavy expenditures for the military, the rate of economic development has not been impressive, and in East Pakistan relative deterioration has occurred. In South Korea, issues of fiscal management have been the source of continuous internal tension among the military ruling group, and to the extent that economic development takes place, it derives from large contributions of United States economic assistance. Egypt is a case of relative success, where, after much experimentation, military rule established an equilibrium between private and public sectors of economic activity by an expansion of the governmental sector, incorporating some of the economic competition features of "Tito-type" state socialism. Industrial establishments are in the hands of civilian managers or former army officers who act as managers, subject to the control of central planning agencies.

New nations suffer from overbureaucratization of economic enterprise, and military intervention can easily serve to compound this problem. If a generalization is possible, it is that the wider the sphere of economic involvement, the less effectively is the military able to perform. As centers of technical training and a source of managerial personnel, and even as managers of specific installations, the military operates with reasonable effectiveness. But in tasks of managing wide sectors of the economy, or supplying central economic direction, it suffers from both the limitations inherent in the profession and sheer deficits of personnel resources.

The contributions of the military to political modernization, it has also been argued, are not only economic; the military also serves as an agent of social change. At a minimum, this implies that the army becomes a device for developing a sense of identity — a social psychological element of national unity — which is especially crucial for a nation which has suffered because of colonialism and which is struggling to incorporate diverse ethnic and tribal groups. At a maximum, this implies that experience in the military gives the officer and enlisted man a perspective which is compatible with, or essential for, economic development.

There can be no doubt that the military has the capacity for education in fundamental literacy and in aspects of citizenship training. The military, when it is not engaged in combat, is a training apparatus whose personnel spend considerable time teaching or being taught. The profession views teaching as an essential qualification for a military leader. In short, every effective soldier, by his very task, must be a teacher.

Moreover, the capacities of the military for developing national identifications derive from the unity of its organizational environment. Its members are aware that they belong to a group which has a unified and indivisible military function. Even the civil service does not contribute as directly to national identification because of the variety of separate organs under its jurisdiction.

Many tasks that the new recruit — enlisted man or officer — must perform are highly anxiety-ridden in comparison with civilian enterprises. Yet the military is better equipped to give the soldier material, organizational, and even psychological resources to deal with the problems that he must face. In the military, as compared with other institutions of a new nation, the probability of equal treatment is greater. The result is a sense of cohesion and social solidarity, because men of various regional and ethnic backgrounds are given a common experience and come to think of themselves as Indians, Egyptians, or Nigerians.

How extensive is the impact of the military as an agency for building a sense of national identity? There are two different aspects to the role of the military as an agency of socialization. On the one hand, there is the direct consequence of military service; and on the other hand, there is the symbolic value of the armed forces for the population as a whole. It is easy to overlook the wide variation in the impact of the military in different new nations. In countries where there have been extensive hostilities or some military tradition, the consequences are deep and important, but in others, especially in Sub-Sahara Africa, the penetration of the military into the social fabric is limited by the size and newness of the armed forces.

Clearly, for those directly involved, military service is a powerful personal experience. Only in Israel, Turkey, and Thailand is there universal military training; in Egypt, there is a modified form of universal military service. In these countries, the military is a device for fundamental education and is undoubtedly significant for a large proportion of the young age groups served. Moreover, in a few countries, personnel are available to assist civilian institutions in fundamental education which contributes greatly to a positive image of the military. For example, the Turkish army in 1962 had 11,000 officer cadets engaged in supporting the government's program against illiteracy.

But in general, new nations' armies are based upon long-term volunteers and therefore involve only a tiny fraction of the population. Independence, moreover, has generally been won without extensive mobilization of the civilian population. Even in a country like India, where the armed services total one-half million, the number of young men who enter military service is so small that plans have been developed for a national youth corps which would emphasize military discipline. Government and political leaders deem such discipline appropriate for modernization, even though such a youth service would not be expected to produce career soldiers.

It is difficult to estimate the extent to which the military operates as a source of self-esteem and ego-enhancement for the population at large. Armies are used for ceremonial purposes and are conspicuously garrisoned in national capitals. They are frequently on display on patriotic holidays and their parades in some countries, for example Indonesia, penetrate into the smallest towns. These are part of the efforts of political leaders — military and civilian — to foster nationalistic feelings, and in these countries the military contributes to the popular sense of self-esteem. In those few countries where the armed forces were extensively involved in national liberation, popular support for the military is widespread. In countries where there are disputed borders, or clear, politically defined enemies, the military moves more into mass consciousness.

But in other new nations, particularly in Sub-Sahara Africa, the mass media make athletic heroes and national sports more significant elements of popular culture than military formations. In these new nations, the sports arena is the most conspicuous building in the national or regional capital. Likewise, some of these military formations, when performing their national duties, are still viewed with distance as "they" rather than "we." In addition, there are still residues of hostility toward these armies because of poor behavior and brutality during the period of de-mobilization after World War II.

If the military serves a "morale-building" function, it is particularly for the small, alert, and politically sensitized middle class. Frequently, and especially in the Middle East, developing positive mass sentiment for the military is an important political task. In other words, the process of modernization requires that popular support be generated for the military, as much as the reverse. Egypt is an example of a country where, in the period of a few years after the military took power, public regard for the military rose because of more equitable procedures for military service, the prestige of the new military politicians, and the generally increased effectiveness of government.

THE MECHANICS OF
POLITICAL INTERVENTION

Earlier, it was assumed that the comparative analysis of the political role of the military, if it is possible at all, hinges on the observation that all new nations desire to become modern. This "universal" goal, in a crude sense, creates a common set of political problems. While the meaning of modernity is either undefined or variously defined, no elite group — except elements of religious leadership — insists on the superiority of tradition per se, if only because traditional society was unable to resist Western influence and the imposition of colonial rule. To be modern is therefore, at a minimum, an essential aspect of being independent. But there is additional common political content in the drive to be modern. No matter what political symbols are emphasized to give substance to the idea of modernity, it seems almost universally to mean, in new nations, the goal of increased economic activity and a higher standard of living. The military, when it becomes an agent of political change, cannot avoid this overriding popular goal. In fact, modernization is a more overriding political objective than establishing a claim to legitimate authority.

Military and civilian leaders speak mainly of modernization, to a lesser extent of industrialization, and they avoid reference to urbanization. But to modernize the economy of a new nation, it is necessary to develop mass participation in new forms of social organization, ranging from village co-operatives to professional associations.

This is what is meant by the phrase "social mobilization." Social mobilization can rely in varying degrees on persuasion or coercion. For the time being, most new nations, including the most Marxist-oriented ones, have not embraced an explicit ideology of the dictatorship of the proletariat which would supply a justification for the mass use of terror as a political instrument. On the other hand, although every new nation, even the poorest one, has at its disposal a mass media system, such means are not adequate for the tasks of social mobilization. If a prime political objective is persuasion rather than coercion, it becomes necessary to judge the effectiveness of a military oligarchy in domestic politics in terms of the military's ability to develop or permit the development of a mass political base. This is what is essentially involved in the last proposition about political intervention. After "takeover," the military regime faces the tasks of supplying national political leadership. If the military is to meet this political goal, it must develop a viable mass political apparatus outside of its organizational structure — but an apparatus which would respond to its dominant influence. The military might be able to achieve the same objectives by transforming itself, but this seems much less feasible. The military oligarchy is also only a partial regime, because of the problems inherent in succession. All regimes have the task of managing succession. But between the need to generate mass political support and the need to solve the problems of political succession, the new nations appear to find the former the overriding consideration.

What factors assist or retard the military in developing an apparatus of mass political support? Social origins, education, and skill help to explain the military's commitment to economic and social modernization. But the same factors inhibit political change, since they highlight the separateness, if not the exclusiveness, of military leaders from other elite groups, especially from political elites. Likewise, as noted above, the format of military organization and the absence of appropriate political skills stand in the way of developing new political devices. An unpolitical ideology operates in the same direction; but in varying degrees the mixture of activism, asceticism, and pragmatism in its orientation predisposes the military at least to recognize the need for developing mass support.

But the "definition of the situation" in which the military officer finds himself becomes as crucial as his social heritage and professional tradition. The situation is defined by the type of "takeover" which transforms the army into a military oligarchy. Earlier, a distinction was made between "designed militarism," the premeditated search for political power, and "reactive militarism," the expansion of military power that results from the weakness of civilian institutions and the pressures of civilians to expand the military role. "Reactive" rather than "designed" militarism is the usual case in the new nations. The Free Officers in Egypt have supplied one of the few examples approximating "designed" militarism. Although Nasser emerged as the personal leader, the organization was of the junta type, involving a key group of perhaps fifty to one hundred central activists who had had extensive contact and political activity. By contrast, Pakistan's would be a clear-cut case of the more typical reactive militarism. The involvement of the military in domestic politics was brought about at the request of key civilian politicians. Top military leadership there had had little experience in domestic politics, although they appear to have had operational plans and adequate intelligence for accomplishing the "takeover." The decision to intervene was made by the top leader and a few trusted confidants, while the military establishment responded as a whole and without any dissent. In reality, many seizures of power are a mixture of both types, in which reactive aspects dominate.

Another crucial aspect of the political definition of the situation is that, for the majority of cases where the military has become the ruling political group, the society had been experimenting with a form of civilian political system with some type of a parliament. A military oligarchy does not arise immediately as colonial governments withdraw; partisan civilian politicians fail first to demonstrate effective leadership or adherence to the "rules of the game." In contrast to these forms of militarism, to date there has not been a case in which an authoritarian-mass one-party system has lost power to the military in a coup d'état. In countries with such systems, top political leadership seems highly sensitive to the role of the military. The military establishments in some of these countries are, perhaps, too new and too limited to effect such a seizure of power. But it does appear that such regimes have capacities for excluding the military from domestic politics by their paramilitary units, secret police, and mass party organization. In this sense, they have already established some of the elements of the totalitarian civil-military model.

It is relevant to note which efforts of the military have failed to bring about a successful seizure of power. In Indonesia, a military coup failed in October, 1952, because of unclear demands by military leaders and lack of internal cohesion among different elements of the army.[5] In Ceylon, the coup of January, 1962, was

[5] Herbert Feith, *The Decline of Constitutional Democracy in Indonesia* (Ithaca, N.Y.: Cornell University Press, 1962), pp. 225–302.

one of the few that failed. It was organized mainly by police officers, although it did have some key military figures representing the relatively small army. In this instance, the police did not appear to have either the necessary organizational capacity or the public image of national interest. This mixed group of leaders could not maintain the necessary secrecy, since the civilian authorities were prematurely informed.

Other failures have been recorded in authoritarian regimes based on personal domination (Ethiopia and South Vietnam). Under these circumstances, the military insurrectionists have greater difficulty than when there is some level of parliamentary procedure in the society. Failure means that the insurrectionary forces have not mobilized sufficient resources or acted forthrightly. But the political instability of these countries implies that the military will again seek to achieve political power.[6]

After the seizure of power, a difference in style of exercising authority emerges as between internal management of the regime and external relations of the regime with other political groups and the population at large. Although military oligarchies are dominated by a leading political personality, the style of internal administration at the highest level is managerial, with a high level of internal negotiation among specialists and administrative leaders. Rustow asserts that the military gave Turkey its first genuine experience of government by discussion.[7] Military procedures of staff work and the style of military administrative leaders help make such arrangements possible. In a fundamental sense, these regimes are not personal military dictatorships. Wherever there is any reliable evidence from Turkey, Burma, Pakistan, Egypt, or Sudan, one finds that the military institutes a form of cabinet government without an electorate. Within the cabinet considerable discussion takes place.

[6] In the very traditional authoritarian-personal system of Yemen, the officers engaged in a coup in September, 1962, and installed Brigadier Abdullah al-Salal.
[7] D. Rustow, "The Army and the Founding of the Turkish Republic," *World Politics* (July, 1959), p. 546.

The military oligarchy must contain any factionalism that develops within the inner circle. Ataturk controlled factionalism by requiring army officers who became active in partisan politics to retire or resign their commissions. Diplomatic exile remains a favorite technique for dissenters or extremists. During the contemporary period of renewed political intervention of the Turkish army, General Cemal Gursel sent fourteen members of the Committee on National Unity, who did not believe in early return to civilian power, to foreign diplomatic posts.[8] When factionalism becomes rife and deep, widespread spying and counterspying develop. Spy systems are extensive in countries like Thailand, and in Sudan dissident officers are closely supervised and dominated by the personalities of the top-ranking two or three officers.

The military approach to civilian political groups and the population at large is often much more repressive and authoritarian, but far short of mass terror. "Takeover" of power leads to some curtailment of freedom of speech and often to repression of newspapers. Tensions between the military and journalists are particularly acute. The military profession views journalists as irresponsible and almost traitorous, since they are continually criticizing.

It is possible to speak of a "cycle of distrust." Repression and mild coercion produce counterresistance. In particular, university student groups become centers of opposition. Burma is a pointed case, where the military joined forces with the police in repressing the Communist-oriented student movement and in demolishing its headquarters building. As counterresistance develops, police and espionage systems are relied upon more heavily and the cycle of distrust deepens and widens.

The political skill of the military oligarchy is put to the test if it seeks to reverse the cycle of distrust. Requirements for economic development, as well as demands of technocratically oriented middle-class groups, press against continued coercion. The professional self-image of the military also contributes to efforts

[8] *The New York Times,* June 3, 1961, p. 29.

to reduce repression. This phase of reversing the cycle of mistrust is beginning to emerge in some of the new nations. Thus, it is instructive to compare efforts in four countries where the military has sought to develop popular support by mass propaganda or by mass political organization: Egypt, Pakistan, South Korea, and Burma. Differences can be drawn between the Egyptian and the Pakistani military ruling groups, for in this comparison it appears that a military group which came into power through "designed militarism," as contrasted with "reactive militarism," is more sensitive to the problems of developing mass political organs.

This is not to conclude that the Egyptians have been particularly successful; it is to say that they have been continuously active in searching for an appropriate solution. Even before the seizure of political power, Nasser declared in his writings that the military could only succeed in its national revolution if it was able to mobilize popular support. Early in its existence as a military oligarchy, the Free Officers Committee began experimenting with a political front group which would serve as a basis for mass organization. The formula for managing political mobilization has been the creation from the top down of a mass organization under the direction of trusted military officers. The national political front was designed to have a complete structure from the village through the national government, incorporating many Soviet-type single-party features. In fact, it appears that the Nasser government relied heavily on advisors from the Tito regime in directing this effort. Nasser has also repeatedly emphasized the importance of elections, although he undoubtedly means them to be symbolic devices for political mobilization.

The first Nasser effort in this direction was the "Liberation Rally" organized in 1954, which made use of personnel from the Ministry of the Interior for organizational field work. In 1956, it was recast into the "National Union" with the mandate that all Egyptians were in effect members. In recognition of the failure of this undifferentiated effort, and because of the movement toward a more socialist type of economy, steps were taken in

1961 and 1962 to create a new format called the "Socialist Union."
The "Socialist Union" was not based on universal membership
but required that members of the "electorate" indicate their desire for membership.

The organizational principle of the "Socialist Union" is twofold;
one, geographical, which means that traditional local elites of the
villages were heavily represented; and two, functional, which
means that the newer urban middle-class professionals and specialists dominated. The whole effort has been handicapped by a lack
of trained party workers. Nevertheless, the "Socialist Union" does
represent a newly created instrument of political mobilization,
with some opportunity for upward social and political communication. A measure of its level of popular involvement is that the
majority of the voting population have registered to become
members. The leaders of the "Socialist Union" are high-ranking
civil servants and political figures who stood for election to the
newly created parliament. At the village level it does permit peasants to confront, if not to challenge, the older political leadership.

In contrast to the one-party system of the Soviet Union, army
personnel as such are not members, and there are no branches
within the army. Former officers who have key civilian posts are
involved in the work of the "Socialist Union," and a number of
such former officers stood for election. In addition, at the very
top, key posts are held by trusted members of the revolutionary
junta. Thus, the whole "Socialist Union" operates on the assumption that the army is the dominant political force.

In Pakistan, the military has much more reluctantly oriented
itself to the necessity of some sort of mass political movement. Its
method has been the slow construction of an organization from
the bottom up. Councils, designed to become points of contact
with the population, have been organized in villages, but there
is no semblance of an effort to integrate these councils into a
national movement. In fact, the movement is relatively undeveloped, and it is essentially an administrative arm of the government. The Ayub government suspended party activity for a

period after the advent of the military government. In October, 1962, a Democratic Front, made up of diverse former parties and political leaders, was permitted partially to emerge. It offered as its platform one aim — the "democratization" of Field Marshal Ayub's constitution, which concentrated powers in the hands of the chief executive. Rather than immediately repress the Democratic Front, the Home Minister, Lieutenant General Mohammed Habibullah Khan, announced that he would seek a Supreme court ruling against the Front activities. These activities revolved around the antimilitary government agitations of former Prime Minister Huseyn Shaheed Suhrawardy, who was released in August, 1962, after serving nearly seven months in an air-conditioned cell in Karachi for his political activities.[9] When it took power, the military government of Pakistan publicly expressed its intention to return the political system to civilian groups at some unspecified time. Nevertheless, it has not been active in the reconstruction of such groups or in encouraging the development of new groups.

In South Korea, the military assumed political control of the civilian government after a period of ineffective civilian parliamentary leadership, climaxed by a student uprising which precipitated a political crisis. The response of the military was reactive, although, once in power, it displayed considerable initiative to change the civilian political system as well as to modernize the country economically. Despite profound economic problems and lack of preparation for its political responsibility, the military oligarchy proceeded on a comprehensive basis and with considerable political skill. No doubt many leading military officers had experienced political activity sponsored by the American military government in South Korea, and these practices influenced their thinking. In addition to the usual procedure of blacklisting traditional and "corrupt" political leaders, they sought to develop, by means of mass propaganda, some popular support for economic modernization and the regime. But the striking aspect of the South

* *New York Times*, November, 1962.

Korean military junta was that it apparently recognized the inherent limitations of the military for mass political organization. Rather than make the army a mass political agency, it took steps to organize a civilian-type mass party. Following the model of Ataturk — knowingly or unknowingly — politically interested officers were urged to resign from active duty and become the cadre of this new party. (The exact number is not known but was probably about one hundred.) The party was designed to supply popular support for General Chung Hee Park, chief of the South Korean military junta, when he would run for election to the post of president. The very existence of this new party, committed to economic modernization and elimination of corruption, made a contribution to political change. Moreover, military leaders sought to conserve their political influence rather than to dissipate it.

In February, 1963, they announced that they would not participate in the forthcoming election if the civilian political leaders agreed to basic reforms. In return for removing the blacklist of political leaders who were denied the right to participate in politics, they required that civilian politicians accept the validity of the student and military revolution, promise no retaliation against new appointments to the civil service, and press ahead with economic reform. This announcement by the military not to participate in the election was conditioned by the failure of its economic currency reform, a widespread crop failure, and the resulting growth of popular hostility. Officials of the Department of State also put the military junta under strong pressure to withdraw. But the South Korean junta sought to maximize its political intervention by limiting its role, as in the case of Turkey, to that of umpire between civilian political parties, including the one it had created. Therefore, it was not surprising when General Park and the South Korean military oligarchy, continuing their search for a political format, decided that he would run as a "civilian" under the sponsorship of the military-created political party.

In Burma, when the military first took over, it promised a speedy return to civilian government after it had "cleaned up the mess."

During this first period, the Burmese army, lacking any mechanism for mass contact, sought to restore the village headmen to positions of authority. In essence, they sought to restore aspects of the older forms of colonial administration. While such efforts were only successful in varying measure, they represent some degree of self-awareness of the political deficiencies of a military oligarchy. In order to protect its organizational integrity and honor its pledges, the Burmese army did withdraw from power and permit the return of civilian government under a popular election, and the army supported the civilian political party that won the election. After internal difficulties increased, the military believed that it once more had to assume power. In assuming power for the second time, the military showed greater concern with mobilizing popular support, but it was not able to take any comprehensive steps toward developing mass organs of social mobilization.

The same dilemmas of military power and the mobilization of popular support operate in Indonesia, where the army acts as a member of a political coalition. Where local commanders find a need to maintain contact with the population at large but lack general military directives, they express their own personal approach to mass political action. A partial explanation of the different responses to mobilizing mass support among these five military groups seems to rest in their prior political contacts and activity. The more extensive their political contacts and political activity before power, the more likely they are to be sensitive to the need for mass political involvement. Sensitivity to these problems, however, is no measure of ability to cope with them.

As the political role of the military broadens domestically, military leaders also find themselves more deeply involved in the management of foreign affairs. The new nations are hardly underdeveloped in their concern with foreign affairs. One striking characteristic of the nationalism that emerges in new nations is that it immediately involves them in the world-wide arena of international politics. The existence of the United Nations, with its membership principle of one nation—one vote, and the realities of

regional politics require each nation, no matter how small, to
embark upon a foreign policy. To profess independence from the
major power blocs seems to be an essential way of demonstrating
that national independence has been achieved. When tiny Cyprus
became an independent republic, Archbishop Makarios' first announcement was that his new republic would be independent
in foreign affairs and "we do not want to let our foreign policy
be declared by either Greece or Turkey." The plunge into foreign
affairs is also a by-product of civilian political leaders who rose
to power through techniques of agitation and who are prepared to
focus national attention on foreign enterprises rather than to confront the internal realities of economic and social development.

James Coleman suggests that the defense policies of new nations
can be characterized as either "single dependency" or "multiple
dependency" nations.[10] The single-dependency nations are those
which continue to maintain a military alliance with their former
colonial power or receive their military assistance from that country. Multiple-dependency nations are those which seek to obtain
military assistance from more than one nation.

Single dependency is a major factor in countries like Turkey,
Pakistan, and Thailand, which are tied to regional security alliances with the United States. Other clear-cut cases of single dependency are the former French colonies of West and Equatorial
Africa that have security pacts with France and maintain close
association with French military forces. But even these French-
speaking new nations are gradually moving toward Africanization
of their forces. In fact, the general trend is toward a decline in
single dependency, for both political and technical reasons. Nigeria, which may be called a single-dependency nation because
it has chosen to maintain close contact with Great Britain, abro-
gated its mutual defense pact in order to further its political
ambitions for leadership among African nations.

Multiple dependency has two purposes. On the one hand, in
countries like Ethiopia, the policy of obtaining military assistance

[10] *Op. cit.*, p. 386.

from a variety of nations has been pursued in order to prevent the development of a cohesive internal military bloc with political power. The other purpose of multiple dependency is to enhance freedom of action in foreign policy and "neutralism" in the world balance of power. Thus Burma and, more recently, India have sought to eliminate dependence of NATO nations as suppliers of military assistance. The Indonesian military force followed a policy of extensive multiple dependency in order to demonstrate its neutrality, although, in balance, most of its armaments have come from the Soviet Union. Indonesian army officers have been trained in the United States, air force officers in Great Britain, and naval officers in various countries in Western Europe. Naval and air force officers have been sent to Communist countries like Poland and Czechoslovakia and even to neutralist countries like Egypt. It remains problematic whether the policies followed by neutralist countries with authoritarian-mass parties, such as Ghana, Mali, and Guinea, are expressions of a multiple-dependency policy or whether, in effect, they will emerge as cases of single-dependency on the Soviet bloc.

Undoubtedly, foreign military assistance and officer training abroad have an impact on the military and its politics, domestic and foreign. But the source from which military assistance or officer training is obtained is only one element in understanding the political orientation of the military of the new nations, and often the consequence is unanticipated. In the past, Great Britain, through its schools in England, has been the major contributor to officer training abroad for the countries of our sample. For example, Gutteridge estimates that about thirty countries have sent officers to Sandhurst.[11] While these personnel are mainly from British Commonwealth nations, they also come from Thailand, Iraq, and Libya. Informally and bilaterally, larger new nations of the Commonwealth are able to contribute to the political military needs of smaller nations who desire sources of assistance aside from the two major power blocs. For example, the Indian

[11] Gutteridge, *op. cit.*, p. 18.

army has training programs for officers from Malaya, Nepal, Indonesia, Burma, and Ethiopia. No doubt, training at these schools has helped to implant the British officer code of personal and professional conduct, although the political implications are much more diffuse. The French trained the original post-World War II South Vietnamese army, and they continued a military link with Cambodia. In both cases, the political influence could best be described as negative in the long run. French influence also operates in its ex-colonies among the nations of Sub-Sahara Africa.

In recent years, the United States has more and more emerged as a country to which new nations send officers for training, especially South Korea, South Vietnam, Thailand, Tunisia, and, to a lesser but still important extent, Indonesia. American training influence is equally strong through military assistance missions which operate in new nations. Since 1947, contingents of American officers have been sent each year to new nations to instruct military personnel in the use of weapons supplied under military assistance programs. Gradually, over the years, United States political and military authorities have become aware that such programs have domestic political implications for new nations. They have become concerned that these programs help develop pro-American loyalties among the officers of new nations. To this end, for example, more than one thousand U.S. military assistance officers were given special training before they were sent abroad.

It is difficult, if not impossible, to judge what type of political perspectives emerge among new nations' officers specifically from their contact with American military and civilian personnel. When officers are sent to weapons training schools located in the southern region of the United States, many become impressed with the extent of racial discrimination. There is ample evidence, however, that new nations' officers sent to the service academies and staff and command schools are deeply touched by the close personal contacts they develop and by the sense of public service they see among cadets and officers. U.S. military assistance officers, operating in the new nations, are personally well received, mainly because they have been carefully selected and are prepared to make themselves useful in day-to-day operational problems. Occasionally an enterprising American officer will seek to develop, in his new-nation counterparts, a sense of the modernizing functions that armies might play; but generally such officers are oriented toward immediate "hardware" military tasks. The concept of "civil action"— the idea that the military is an agent of development — has not become a pervasive outlook in these military assistance programs, except recently in the case of South Vietnam.

Likewise, interpersonal relations do not supply a basis for communication about U.S. political and strategic intention. The personnel of new nations develop their images of foreign affairs from other sources, mainly from their own military leadership. U.S. military assistance personnel operating in new nations are either not prepared or not inclined to deal with basic questions of the political responsibility of the military in new nations. This is defined as a political matter within the jurisdiction of the Department of State and embassy personnel, who have no — or few — operating contacts with the military. As a result, U.S. military assistance programs do not supply a stimulus of officers in new nations to think creatively about the potentials and limitations of the military's role in the development of their countries. In recent years the Soviet Union has entered the field, both with extensive military assistance training programs in new nations and with limited officer training programs at home, as for example in Ghana. Almost nothing is known about the political impact of these training programs on new nations' officers.

The link between foreign and domestic politics in a new nation is obviously broader than the sources of military assistance and officer training. In fact, foreign military assistance is often only partially related to American or Soviet dependency and more related to national expansionist objectives. Few new nations are immune from some immediate security problem, either real or imagined. But issues of border disputes and even clashes of interest among new nations are, in turn, overshadowed by the goals

of eliminating vestiges of colonial rule, with great potential consequence in Sub-Sahara Africa, South and Southeast Asia, and,
to a much lesser extent, North Africa.

African officers see the Republic of South Africa emerging as
a vague but potential military objective. The pressure of the
apartheid policy has the countereffect of encouraging internal
terror movements. Outside support for these movements, plus
guerrilla and irregular conflict, combined with political agitation,
are likely first steps, and the tension has already gone beyond
the threshold level. Already Angola serves as a Negro equivalent
to the Arabic mobilization for Algeria. Ghana, Israel, Algeria, and
the Congo governments have already supplied military and paramilitary support. While the conventional military ratios are overwhelmingly in favor of the Nationalists in South Africa, and will
remain so for a number of years, there is no reason to believe that
African professional officers will resist the temptation to threaten
with their weapons and engage in token demonstrations to liberate
their oppressed brethren.

In Southeast Asia, vestiges of colonialism present limited but
equally appropriate targets for new nations' expansionism. The
focal point is the British-supported effort to create a Malaysian
political entity. Even the relatively stable and democratically controlled Philippines has joined Indonesia in this expansionist policy.
The military forces of both nations are sufficient to make their
threats and expansionist claims credible.

These various expansionist moves give rise to ambitious political-military alliances which mainly express national rivalries and
the struggle for prestige. The Arab League, the oldest, has to date
failed in its objective of preventing the establishment of a sovereign state of Israel. It has been transformed into a forum for
national rivalries among participating members. The Egyptian
military oligarchy came into power with strong pan-Arabic aspirations. While it has not abandoned its pan-nationalist interests, it
has clearly become more realistic about its foreign policy goals,
since the collapse of the union with Syria. By means of military

intervention on behalf of the officer revolt in Yemen, and through political support of military and socialist elements in Iraq and Syria, Egypt continues its pan-nationalist activities. In Africa, both North Africa and the Sub-Sahara, there have been persistent efforts to create regional blocs with military overtones. The so-called Casablanca powers have sought to establish their own pro-African anticolonial military organization with the format of the North Atlantic Treaty Organization (Egypt, Ghana, Guinea, Mali, Algeria, and Morocco). In 1961, Accra was designated the location of the joint military high command, and Thami Wazanni of Morocco was appointed as secretary-general, with General Mohammad Fawzi of the Egyptian army, a veteran of the Palestinian war, as the military commander. Members of this Casablanca group, particularly under the stimulation of Kwame Nkrumah, have held conferences on the demilitarization of Africa and international nuclear arms control. In opposition to the Casablanca group, Tunisia, Sudan, Nigeria, Ethiopia, Togo, Liberia, and Cameroun have informally and by means of their United Nations contacts sought to express their middle-of-the-road position. Also in competition with the Casablanca group have been Haile Selassie's efforts to establish a pan-African freedom movement involving East, Central, and South African groups. In February, 1962, a conference was held at which he asserted that members of an East African alliance would not hesitate to defend each other's rights nor withdraw from the "struggle for total liberation of Africa." While these activities are more symbolic than realistic, they indicate that the new nations do not intend to forego international power politics as it is traditionally played.

United Nations military operations in the Middle East, the Congo, and subsequently in New Guinea, present the new nations with an opportunity to engage in regional balance-of-power politics within a new and legal format. As the new nations have increased their role in the administrative secretariat of the United Nations, the position of military adviser has been given to an Indian, Brigadier Jit Rikhye, who represents the prototype of a

United Nations military officer, having seen duty in the Gaza Strip
and in the Congo. As a result, he was placed in charge of military
aspects of U.N. intervention in the transition of New Guinea to
Indonesia.

Thus, the mechanics of political intervention of the military in
the new nations, as in the old nations, involve both domestic and
foreign policy. Clearly, domestic issues and domestic political
objectives are overriding, but new nations continue to prepare
for military intervention in support of foreign policy objectives.
If the task of creating a domestic political apparatus to assist economic modernization seems to present a formidable objective to
military oligarchies, and is yet to be solved adequately, the political requirement to support a positive foreign policy can only
complicate the tasks of political change.

THE PRECONDITIONS FOR
POLITICAL BALANCE

It appears to be a universal political conception that a new state
requires an army. In the course of this study, it was hoped that at
least some new nations would make it national policy not to create
an army, or at least de facto to rely on a mobile police force. It
would be revealing to see what kind of internal political balance
emerged in a new nation without an army. In effect, it turned
out that there is no such new nation in our sample. Even the 200-
man army of Togo was capable of political intervention by the
use of force. No political leader of a new nation has openly declared that his country can operate as an independent nation without a military establishment. In fact, one is even struck by the
absence of extensive public discussion in new nations about the
possibility of relying on an armed police force instead of a conventional army. Only Prime Minister Julius Nyerere, of Tanganyika, has been reported as commenting on this possibility.[12] The
existence of the United Nations has not been able to remove tensions and conflicts about national borders from the agenda of

[12] Gutteridge, op. cit., p. 6.

international relations, even in Sub-Sahara Africa where the possibility of such agreements were perhaps the most likely. To the contrary, as mentioned above, the existence of the United Nations has created pressures for a national army.

It could be argued that if a new nation elected not to have an army, its mobile police force would serve as an equivalent instrument of potential political intervention. Such a police force might be even more disruptive to the internal political balance. There are no real answers to such a hypothetical question. Mobile police force would clearly be less costly. The police, however, would be more likely to rely on local coercive pressure, and they would have less of a sense of national goals. In fact, it might be argued that, in the absence of an army as a counterforce, the police would tend to expand their political power in new nations with weak political institutions, and their intervention might be highly unstable and fragmentary. Thus, while it might have been an important political experiment to develop some new nations without armies, there is no guarantee that such arrangements would be uniformly superior. In any case, it is not possible to believe that new nations could have been stimulated in this direction by the major powers. Thus, in exploring the relevance of democratic theory for the politics of new nations, one must take the military, both realistically and theoretically, as a core institution.

Writers concerned with the classical theory of democracy have in the past asserted that the political neutrality of the military is an essential component of a democratic political system. This requirement has been reformulated, but not because contemporary political theorists have retreated under the pressure of international relations and political realities. Because they have developed a clearer notion of the institutional requirements for a democratic society, political theorists have come to believe that a theory of democratic consent must also encompass the military.

When the model of democratic civil-military relations was initially set forth in this analysis, the military was hardly seen as neutral. For it to be neutral would, in effect, mean that military personnel were no more or less than hired mercenaries. The self-conception of a mercenary military is at variance with the political morality of modern nationalism. Too often, political neutrality in the military is disguised opposition to democratic principles. Instead, in terms of democratic theory, the military needs to be committed to the basic format of a democratic political system, even though it must remain non-partisan in domestic politics. It must have a political orientation and, in fact, a political education similar to that of the citizenry at large — one that enables it to act within the broad consensus of the polity.

In this reformulated sense, the political theory of the democratic model of civil-military relations has application to the political goals of a new nation. Therefore, the basis on which the military broadens its political involvement becomes a central issue. Is the military's political activity an expression of its fundamental commitment to the emerging values of the society?

At this point, some normative concepts must be introduced. If this essay has avoided emphasizing terms like "political development" and "political modernization," some equivalent concept of political goals is required. These terms are too closely parallel to economic analysis to encompass all of the ideological, moral, and organizational tasks which demand solution. They have all the overtones of the "idea of progress" as a legacy of Western political experience. On the other hand, such terms do serve some positive purpose. They help to question the appropriateness of existing political institutions for economic and social tasks at hand, and thereby create groundwork for new intellectual contributions.

Edward Shils speaks of the normative concept of "tutelary democracy" as the appropriate political goal for new nations. Such a concept has strong ideological overtones. But an intellectual contribution to political development must be grounded in a set of values. No single concept will suffice as a basis for evaluating the political objectives and performance of the military. Instead, it is necessary to grope for a variety of criteria of performance. Such a set of criteria would include the capacity of the political system to generate social and economic change, but would have, as its basic dimension, the minimization of coercion. To achieve this goal, there must be developed a mass political organization which permits extensive internal communication and bargaining between different organized groups. In varying degrees, there is more than one model of civil-military relations which can contribute to such political development.

It is not an exaggeration to conclude from this analysis of the military profession in the new nations that contemporary civil-military patterns are essentially transitional. The search for an orderly military life does not supply a simple formula for a viable political system. First, the authoritarian-personal type of control, as in the case of Ethiopia, is a format which cannot produce the conditions for modernization and which seems certain to be swept aside by some form of collective leadership – civilian or, more likely, military. Second, in authoritarian-mass party nations, as for example Ghana, the civilian political regimes appear to have an organizational capacity to rule and to keep the military confined in its political role. But this approach, because of its ideological assumptions and coercive practices, fails to articulate with the objectives and long-term goals of a tutelary democracy. The number of new nations in this model – with varying degrees of leftist and Soviet orientation – is likely to increase if other types of political control fail. Third, the democratic-competitive control of civilian leadership, including some forms of quasi-competitive elections, for example, as in India and Malaya, is indeed fragile and subject to extreme internal and external pressure. But there are still enough examples to make it a political reality for new nations. The fourth and fifth types – the military as coalition partner, or the military as ruling oligarchy – have the same political task: to help create some sort of mass apparatus which makes possible the shaping of a minimum level of political consensus.

The focus of this analysis has been on the internal organization of the military profession, in part by a comparison of new with old nations, and in part, by seeking contrasts among the new nations. By way of summary, the military of the new nations are more politicized than their Western counterparts, and they may even produce a cadre of political activists. The process of recruitment, education, and the attendant emergence of professional cohesion all work to support this politicalization of the military. Life career and indoctrination lead its personnel to a broad identification with national interest. But the military does not have appropriate political ideologies. While they are strongly nationalistic, oriented to collective and governmental enterprise, military officers are skeptical and even hostile to organized politics, especially as practiced by partisan political groups. They must learn the meaning of politics by actual experience. Even the internal cohesion of the military profession is bought at the expense of a sense of identification with politicians as a leadership group. This is not to overlook the fact that military officers who have kinship ties with civilian and political leaders may seek out individual officers. What is lacking in new nations is a basis of mutual trust between politicians and the military profession.

Yet, pressure toward political involvement does not necessarily imply the development of appropriate skills for the broader roles that the military accumulates. In fact, it is most difficult, if not impossible, for the military to manage the politics of a nation in the process of rapid economic development. At best, whether the military operates as a political bloc or as the ruling group, the greater its internal cohesion the greater the likelihood that it can prevent the fragmentation of its political power by means of countercoups.

But the military must be able to do more than merely conserve its power. In the recent past, Turkey, under Ataturk, represented the one case in which a military oligarchy, under an enlightened leader, made fundamental contributions to social and economic modernization. The process of modernization in Turkey was rooted in gradual change and built on evolving institutions. Turkey, as an "older" new nation, had a period of development which

seems longer that what the "newer" new nations have set for themselves. From the beginning of his national leadership, Ataturk
had a sharp sense of the limits of the military in politics. He
seemed to look forward to some form of party rule over which the
military would be the arbiter. As mentioned above, perhaps his
most decisive step was to insist that army officers who wanted to
become directly involved in partisan politics — as opposed to na-
tion-building — had to leave the armed forces. Thus, the military
could maintain its basic cohesion and not suffer the excessive
liabilities that direct political involvement produces.

As the military leaders of the new nations approach the problems of political development, they have the model of Ataturk.
(Some new nations' leaders also see relevant elements in the Tito
regime.) Their timetable may be more pressing, but they have
the advantage of his historical experiment. And there can be no
doubt that the history of Ataturk is not lost on military leaders,
as they struggle for new political forms which might permit the
military to operate as a political umpire rather than as a ruling
oligarchy. And in turn, each relatively successful political accomplishment by a military establishment along these lines helps to
strengthen the viability of the Ataturk concept. When one exam-
ines the military oligarchies currently in power and seeks to
explain their political awareness and their actual efforts to limit
their political involvement, traditional sociological categories of
social background seem less important as explanations than educational and career experiences. Even these factors hardly give
satisfactory answers. It seems as if the concrete intellectual and
political experiences of key officers give political content to the
underlying pragmatism that the military profession engenders.

Thus, if it is possible to give meaning to the term "political assistance," it implies imparting on an intellectual basis the successful experiences of military oligarchies that have been able to limit
their political involvement. Mutual assistance among new nations
will be as important as the influence of the superpowers. It requires, in turn, the training of political organizers — top, middle-

level, and grass-roots agents — just as economic assistance requires the training of industrial and agricultural personnel.

There are, of course, other paths by which modern military managers may withdraw to their barracks. As yet, no new nation has fallen to an outright Communist mass political movement which would neutralize the political power of the military; but there are new nations, particularly Indonesia, where this is possible. More likely, the disruptive consequences of internal factionalism within the military oligarchy will first destroy its ability to rule and pave the way for the rise of militant authoritarian movements, left-wing and right-wing. The process of military intervention is not irreversible, but if political change must wait for the breakdown of a military oligarchy, its outcome will not be conducive to an orderly and humane process of modernization.

APPENDIX

SOCIOLOGICAL NOTES ON THE ANALYSIS
OF MILITARY ELITES [1]

The analysis of patterns of stratification of elites is a theoretical prerequisite for a more comprehensive understanding of modern social structure. A historical and comparative approach is an empirical prerequisite for designing and implementing research on elites. In relating the analysis of elites to social organization, at least four basic considerations must be kept in mind.

1. Analyses of elite groups focus attention on those members of a skill or profession who have achieved leading hierarchical positions. Whereas formal criteria of office, public recognition, or public achievement permit the initial delimitation of an elite, functional criteria are required for redefining the membership. These functional criteria identify those who wield influence without formal office or public recognition. They can be selected junior members of high influence in a hierarchy who have not yet achieved high office. Likewise, they can be specialized per-

[1] This Appendix has been adapted from "Social Stratification and the Comparative Analysis of Elites," *Social Forces*, October, 1956, pp. 81–85; and "Military Elites and the Study of War," *Conflict Resolution*, March, 1957, pp. 9–18. (Material from *Social Forces* is used with permission of the University of North Carolina Press; that from *Conflict Resolution* with permission of the publishers.)

sonnel who are indirectly influential and will have little chance of achieving high office; for example, the private secretaries of political leaders and the public-relations advisers of businessmen. Likewise, there are those who need to be excluded despite their formal rank or station because they have ceased to exercise influence.

The criteria of formal office — rank and position — are generally available and accessible to the social scientist. However, the identification of the informal elite membership is more difficult if it is not to proceed on purely arbitrary and circumstantial grounds. Likewise, the identification of the members of an elite group is more feasible to the degree that the elite is entrenched and has historical continuity. Emergent elites and counter-elites are obviously less discernible on the basis of formal characteristics. Therefore, the identification of elite groups on the basis of formal characteristics alone is likely to underrepresent emergent groups. There can be no doubt that social research to date on the stratification of elites has tended to emphasize formalized elites and therefore to concern itself with the status quo.[2]

2. In the search to explain patterns of elite behavior, the crucial assumption has generally been made that an elite or a counter-elite can be meaningfully described in terms of the social origins and the social backgrounds of its members. The term *social profile* can be employed to designate the uniformities in patterns of social background, social status, and prestige of an elite group. Together with *career patterns* — the uniformities in educational and occupational backgrounds — the constituent variables in elite social stratification come into focus.

But the elite group itself is not completely homogeneous; rather, it too has an internal differentiation.[3] It seems necessary at least

[2] For a detailed analysis of segments of Communist counter-elite groups see Gabriel Almond, *The Appeals of Communism* (Princeton, N.J.: Princeton University Press, 1954).

[3] Compare H. Gerth, "The Nazi Party, Its Leadership and Composition," *American Journal of Sociology*, XLV (1940), 511–41, which analyzes various strata of the party hierarchy, with H. R. Trevor-Roper, *The Last Days of Hitler* (London: Macmillan, 1947). Roper focuses on the inner nucleus of the Nazi Party which surrounded Hitler.

to make a distinction between an elite "cadre" and an elite "nucleus." The elite cadre is the top membership of a skill group or a large-scale organization. It is the group composed of specialists in the specific and technical ends of the organization, and their position is achieved because of these skills. From this elite cadre, the elite nucleus is recruited. They are the very small group of prime leaders who hold the highest posts in the establishment. They are oriented toward the broadest social issues, including innovation, self-scrutiny, and interrelations with other elites. It is the group in whose hands rest the development and the decline of their respective organizations. The elite cadre and the smaller elite nucleus may display markedly different social profiles and career lines. Here we have the difference between the top cadre of technical personnel in manufacturing firms and the market-oriented managers. In the military establishment, here is the difference between the effective regimental and divisional commanders and the politically oriented strategists. An understanding of the interaction and tension between these levels is crucial for the understanding of the stratification of any elite group.

3. The differentiation of one elite group from another is a function of the division of labor. Because of rapid social change and the development of large-scale social organization, the distinction between crucial elite groups tends to be blurred. The movement of personnel between business and government and politics has often been noted in advanced industrialized nations. In totalitarian states, the link between the political party apparatus, the state police, and the security services of the army is such as almost to obliterate institutional lines. The ideal type of the public bureaucrat, the soldier, and the businessman do not necessarily remain clear-cut categories.[4] Overlap in affiliation is as important a dimension of elite behavior as is actual movement from one group to another. To study elites along purely institutional lines would be to overlook the career patterns of the types who bear

[4] To point to these trends is not to imply that a single managerial type emerges, the hypothesis of James Burnham in *The Managerial Revolution* (New York: John Day, 1941).

the burden of interinstitutional co-ordination. As a result, it is often the case that elite groups — especially highly bureaucratized ones — act in terms of personal cliques and factions. These cliques and factions cut across formal bureaucratic arrangements within and between nations. Thereby, elite groups articulate themselves through primary groups.

4. Finally, we are concerned with the forms of power and social control that elite and professional groups exercise. The social-stratification basis of their power cannot be analyzed only in terms of their common *social profiles* and *career patterns*. Organized indoctrination and historical experience converts the constituent human beings into effective social groups. Thus, the uniformities of *indoctrination and ideology* as well as of *self-conceptions and motivations* are concepts that need to be considered in describing the mechanisms by which elite groups maintain themselves and their social stratification. These variables arise from dynamic psychology.[5] But they can well be translated into a social organizational analysis without the resort to crude eclecticism. It is necessary to keep in mind that elite groups have primary group structures through which the uniformities of indoctrination, self-conception, and motivation operate. The traditional categories of analysis of social stratification — income, occupation, prestige, skill, knowledge, social origins, and the like — take on meaning only through an analysis of these primary group and informal influence structures.

The study of military elites in industralized nations is bound by these considerations and requires a concern for those political elites which articulate with military institutions. It is possible to identify different models of political-military elite organization — models which reflect different social structures? Can the consequences of the vast technological developments in warmaking for the organization of elites be traced out, in order to infer emerging trends? Can important uniformities in the motivational and

---

[5] "Psychopathology and Politics" in *The Political Writing of Harold D. Lasswell* (Glencoe, Ill.: Free Press, 1951).

ideological components of differing political and military elites be established?

MODELS OF POLITICAL-MILITARY ELITES

First, it is appropriate to identify in some detail four models of political-military elites — aristocratic, democratic, totalitarian, and garrison state. For a base line, it seems appropriate to speak of the aristocratic model of political-military elite structure. The *aristocratic model* is a composite estimate of Western European powers before industrialism had its full impact.[6] In the aristocratic model, civilian and military elites are socially and functionally integrated. The narrow base of recruitment for both elites and a relatively monolithic power structure provide the civilian elite with a comprehensive basis for political control of the military. Samuel Huntington describes this type of control as a "subjective control" of the military.[7]

There is a rigorous hierarchy in the aristocratic model which delineates both the source of authority and the prestige of any member of the military elite. The low specialization of the military profession makes it possible for the political elite to supply the bulk of the necessary leadership for the military establishment. The classic pattern is the aristocratic family which supplies one son to politics and one to the military. Birth, family connections, and common ideology insure that the military will embody the ideology of the dominant groups in society. Political control is civilian control only because there is an identity of interest between aristocratic and military groups. The military is responsible because it is a part of the government.

In contrast to the aristocratic model stands the democratic one. Under the democratic model the civilian and military elites are

[6] Alfred Vagts, *The History of Militarism* (New York: W. W. Norton & Co., 1937).
[7] "Civilian Control of the Military: A Theoretical Statement," in Heinz Eulau, Samuel Eldersveld, and Morris Janowitz (eds.), *Political Behavior: A Reader in Theory and Research* (Glencoe, Ill.: Free Press, 1956), pp. 380–85.

sharply differentiated. The civilian political elites exercise control over the military through a formal set of rules. Huntington called this type of control "objective control" of the military. These rules specify the functions of the military and the conditions under which the military may exercise its power. Military officers are professionals in the employ of the state. They are a small group, and their careers are distinct from the civilian careers. In fact, being a professional soldier is incompatible with playing any other significant social or political role. The military leaders obey the government because it is their duty and their profession to fight. They are supposed to be committed broadly to national and political goals of a democracy. Professional ethics as well as democratic parliamentary institutions guarantee civilian political supremacy.

The *democratic model* is not a historical reality but rather an objective of political policy. Elements of the democratic model have been achieved only in certain Western industrialized countries, since it requires extremely viable parliamentary institutions and broad social consensus about the ends of government. The democratic model assumes that military leaders can be strongly motivated by professional ethics, and this is most difficult. Paradoxically enough, certain types of officers with aristocratic background have made important contributions to the development of the democratic model.

In the absence of a development toward the democratic model, historical change replaces the aristocratic model with a totalitarian one.[8] The totalitarian model, as it developed in Germany, in Russia, and to a lesser degree in Italy, rests on a form of subjective control, as did the older aristocratic model. But the subjective control of the totalitarian model arises not from any natural or social unity of the political and military elites. On the contrary, a revolutionary political elite of relatively low social status and based on an authoritarian mass political party fashions a new

[8] Hans Speier, *War and the Social Order: Papers in Political Sociology* (New York: G. W. Stewart, 1952).

APPENDIX   189

type of control of the military elite. The revolutionary elite, bedecked with paramilitary symbols and yet forced into temporary
alliance with older military professionals, is dedicated to reconsti-
tuting the military elites. Subjective control of the totalitarian
variety is enforced by the secret police, by party members infil-
trating into the military hierarchy, by arming its own military
units, and by controlling the system of officer selection. Under
subjective control of the totalitarian variety the organizational
independence of the professional military is destroyed.[9]

The *garrison-state model*, as offered by Professor Harold D.
Lasswell, is the weakening of civil supremacy which can arise even
in an effective democratic structure.[10] While the end result of the
garrison state approximates aspects of the totalitarian model,
the garrison state has a different natural history. It is, however,
not the direct domination of politics by the military. Since modern
industrial nations cannot be ruled merely by the political domination of a single small leadership bloc, the garrison state is not
a throwback to a military dictatorship. It is the end result of the
ascent to power of the military elite under conditions of prolonged
international tension. Internal freedom is hampered, and the preparation for war becomes overriding. The garrison state is a new
pattern of coalition in which military groups directly and indirectly wield unprecedented amounts of political and administrative power. The military retains its organizational independence,
provided that it makes appropriate alliances with civil political
factions.

It cannot be assumed that all forms of militarism involve "designed militarism." "Designed militarism"—the type identified
with Prussian militarism—involves the modification and destruction of civilian institutions by military leaders acting directly and

---

[9] The totalitarian model which developed in Western Europe is not the
same as the survival of feudal-like military dictatorship still found in parts
of South America, in which a military junta directly dominates civilian and
military life. The Perón model was a strange combination of the old-style military dictatorship plus the newer devices of the totalitarian model.

[10] "The Garrison State," *American Journal of Sociology*, January, 1941,
pp. 455–68.

premeditatedly through the state and other institutions. Equally significant and more likely to account for crucial aspects of the garrison state, as well as for contemporary American problems, is "unanticipated militarism." "Unanticipated militarism" develops from a lack of effective traditions and practices for controlling the military establishment, as well as from a failure of civilian political leaders to act relevantly and consistently. Under such circumstances a vacuum is created which not only encourages an extension of the tasks and power of military leaderships but actually forces such trends.

The threats to the democratic model cannot be meaningfully analyzed merely from the point of view of "designed militarism." "Designed militarism" emphasizes the impact of military leadership on the civil social structure. "Unanticipated militarism" requires an analysis of the manner in which the military profession responds to the developments in civilian society. The technology of war, which is the advanced technology of civilian society, lies at the root and sets the preconditions in the trends toward "unanticipated militarism."

CONSEQUENCES OF TECHNOLOGICAL TRENDS

In industrialized nations the long-term technological development of war and warmaking required the professionalization of the military elite. Such technological developments were compatible with the democratic model of political-military elites, since this model rests on the differentiation of the functions of politicians and soldiers. However, the current continuous advance in the technology of war begins to weaken the possibility of the democratic elite model.

The vast proliferation of the military establishments of the major industrialized nations is a direct consequence of the continuous development of the technology of warfare. The "permanent" character of these vast military establishments is linked to the "permanent" threat of war. It is well recognized that under these conditions the tasks that military leaders perform tend to widen. Their technological knowledge, their direct and indirect power, and their heightened prestige result in their entrance, of necessity, into arenas which have in the recent past have been reserved for civilian and professional politicians. The result is tremendous stress on the traditional assumptions about the effectiveness of the democratic model for regulating political-military relations. The need that political leaders have for active advice from professional soldiers about the strategic implications of technological change serves only to complicate the task of redefining spheres of competence and responsibility. Totalitarian, as well as democratic, nations are faced with these problems.

The impact of the technological development of warfare over the last half-century leads to a series of propositions about social change in industrialized nations:

1. A larger percentage of the national income of modern states is spent on preparation for, execution of, and repair of the consequences of war.

2. There is more nearly total popular involvement in the consequences of war and war policy, since the military establishment is responsible for the distribution of a larger share of civilian values and since the destructiveness of war has increased asymptotically.

3. The monopoly of legal armed violence by the military has resulted in a decline of the task of suppressing internal violence, as compared with the external tasks of the national security.[11]

4. The rate of technological change has become accelerated, and a wider diversity of skill is required to maintain the military establishment.

5. The previous periodic character of the military establishment (rapid expansion, rapid dismantlement) has given way to a more permanent maintenance or expansion.

6. The permanent character of the military establishment has removed one important source of political-military conflict, i.e., the civilian tendency to abandon the military establishment after

[11] Katherine Chorley, *Armies and the Art of Revolution* (London: Faber & Faber, 1943).

a war. Instead, because of the high rate of technological change, internal conflicts between segments of the military elite have been multiplied.

7. The diversification and specialization of military technology have lengthened the time of formal training required for mastery of military technology, with the result that the temporary citizen army will become less important and a completely professional army more vital.

8. The complexity of the machinery of warfare and the requirements for research, development, and technical maintenance tend to weaken the line of organization between the military and the non-military.

Because of these technological and large-scale administrative developments, civilian society as well as the military establishment is undergoing basic transformation. The contemporary tension in political-military organization within the major industrialized powers has a common basis to the degree that the technological requirements of war are universal. Yet the differences in the amount or character of political power exercised by military leaders and the methods for resolving conflicts between political and military leaders as between the major nation-states cannot be explained primarily, or even to any great extent, by differences in the technological organization of their armed forces. This is not to deny that each weapon system — land, naval, or air — tends to develop among its military managers characteristic orientations toward politics based on the technical potentialities of their weapons. The political outlook of any military establishment will be influenced by whether it is an organization dominated by army, navy, or air force. Nevertheless, technological developments merely set the limits within which the civilian and military elites will share power. National differences in the influence patterns of military elites must be linked to national differences in social structure and elite organization.

These technological trends in war-making have necessitated extensive common modification in the military profession in both democratic and totalitarian systems, regardless of national and cultural differences. The changes in the military reflect organizational requirements which force the permanent military establishment to parallel large-scale civilian organizations. As a result, the military takes on more and more the common characteristics of a government or business organization. Thereby, the differentiation between the military and the civilian — an assumed prerequisite for the democratic elite model — is seriously weakened. In all these trends the model of the professional soldier is being changed by "civilianizing" the military elite to a greater extent than the civilian elite is "militarized."

What are some of these modifications in the military profession? They include (*a*) "democratization" of the officer recruitment base, (*b*) a shift in the basis of organization authority, and (*c*) a narrowing of the skill differential between military and civilian elites. Propositions concerning these trends for the United States military during the last fifty years are applicable in varying form to the military establishment of other major industrialized nations.[12]

a) "DEMOCRATIZATION" OF THE OFFICER RECRUITMENT BASE

Since the turn of the century the top military elites of the major industrialized nations have been undergoing a basic social transformation. The military elites have been shifting their recruitment from a narrow, relatively high-status social base to a broader, lower-status, and more representative social base.

The broadening of the recruitment base reflects the demand for large numbers of trained specialists. As skill becomes the basis of recruitment and advancement, "democratization" of selection and mobility increases. This is a specific case of the general trend in modern social structure to shift from criteria of ascription to those of achievement. In Western Europe the "democratization" of the military elites displaced the aristocratic monopoly of the officer

[12] Morris Janowitz, *The Professional Soldier and Political Power: A Theoretical Orientation and Selected Hypotheses* (Ann Arbor: University of Michigan; Bureau of Government, Institute of Public Administration, 1953).

corps; in the United States an equivalent process can be observed, although social lines are generally less stratified and more fluid. The sheer increase in size of the military establishment contributes to this "democratization." The United States Air Force, with its large demand for technical skill, offered the greatest opportunity for rapid advancement.

From the point of view of the democratic model, "democratization" of social recruitment of military leaders is not necessarily accompanied by "democratization" of outlook and behavior. By "democratization of outlook and behavior" is meant an increase in accountability or an increase in the willingness to be accountable. In fact, the democratization of the military profession carries with it certain opposite tendencies. The newer strata are less aware of the traditions of the democratic model. Their opportunities for mobility make them impatient and demanding of even greater mobility. Their loyalty to the military establishment begins to depend more and more on the conditions of employment rather than on commitment to the organization and its traditions.

The increased representativeness of social background of the military profession also results in an increased heterogeneity of the top leaders within the various military services. Under these conditions it is more difficult to maintain organizational effectiveness and at the same time enforce the norms of civilian political control. (In a totalitarian society, it likewise becomes more difficult to maintain organizational effectiveness and enforce party loyalty.) Of course, any large-scale organization develops devices for overcoming these forms of disruption. The military profession has emphasized honor as a unifying ideology, and intraservice marriage patterns have been a power device for assimilating newcomers into the military establishment. But requirements of bureaucratic efficiency corrode honor, and military marriage, like civilian marriage, is currently more limited in its ability to transmit traditions.

Even more fundamental, the new "democratization" changes the prestige position of the military profession. The older, tradi-

tional soldier has his social prestige regulated by his family of
origin and by the civilian stratum from which he came. What society thought was of little importance as long as his immediate
circle recognized his calling. This was true even in the democratic
model. The British officer corps, with its aristocratic and landed-
gentry background and its respectable middle-class service families, is the classic case in point. In varying degrees before World
War II it was true for the United States Navy, with its socialite
affiliations, and even the United States Army, with its southern
military-family traditions. But with democratization of the profession, the pressure develops for prestige recognition by the public at large. A public-relations approach must supplant a set of
personal relations. Public relations becomes not merely a task for
those specialists assigned to developing public support for military
establishment policies. Every professional soldier, like every businessman or government official, must represent his establishment
and work to enhance the prestige of the professional military. In
turn, a military figure becomes a device to enhance a civilian
enterprise.

b) SHIFT IN THE BASIS OF ORGANIZATION AUTHORITY

It is common to point out that military organization is rigidly
stratified and authoritarian in character because of the necessities
of command. Moreover, since military routines are highly standardized, it is generally asserted that promotion is in good measure
linked to compliance with existing procedures and existing goals
of the organization. (These characteristics are found in "civilian"
bureaucracies but supposedly not with the same high concentration and rigidity.) Once an individual has entered into the military establishment, he has embarked on a career within a single
pervasive institution. Short of withdrawal, he thereby loses the
"freedom of action" that is associated with occupational change
in civilian life.

From such a point of view, the professional soldier is thought
to be authoritarian in outlook. Status and the achievement of

status are thought to be fundamental motivations. The organizing principle of authority is domination — the issuing of direct commands. The professional soldier is seen as limited in his ability and skill to participate in "civilian" political affairs which require flexibility, negotiation, and the "art of persuasion."

It is not generally recognized, however, that a great deal of the military establishment resembles a civilian bureaucracy, as it deals with problems of research, development, supply, and logistics. Even in those areas of the military establishment which are dedicated primarily to combat or to the maintenance of combat readiness, a central concern of top commanders is not the enforcement of rigid discipline but rather the maintenance of high levels of initiative and morale. This is a crucial respect in which the military establishment has undergone a slow and continuing change since the origin of mass armies and rigid military discipline.[13]

Initiative rather than the enforcement of discipline is a consequence of the technical character of modern warfare, which requires highly skilled and highly motivated groups of individuals. Often these formations must operate as scattered and detached units, as opposed to the solid line of older formations. It is also a consequence of the recruitment policies of modern armies, which depend on representative cross-sections of the civilian population rather than on volunteers. Modern armies increasingly draw their recruits from urbanized and industrialized populations and less from illiterate agricultural groups, for whom response to discipline is a crucial and effective form of control. Tolerance for the discomforts of military life decreases. The "rationality" and skepticism of urban life carry over into military institutions to a greater degree than in previous generations. The rationalization of military life makes it necessary to supply more explicit motives. Social relations, personal leadership, material benefits, ideological indoctrination, and the justice and meaningfulness of war aims are now all component parts of morale.

[13] S. L. A. Marshall, *Men Against Fire: The Problem of Battle Command in Future War* (New York: William Morrow & Co., 1947).

Short of complete automation, specialized units manning the crucial technical instruments of war must display fanatically high morale in order to achieve successful military offensive action. Although military formations are still organized on the basis of discipline, military command involves an extensive shift from domination to manipulation as a basis of authority. Manipulation implies persuasion, negotiation, and explanation of the ends of the organization. Direct orders give way to the command conference. Since manipulation involves high social interaction, differences in status are tempered by morale objectives, Shifts from domination to manipulation, from status to morale, are present in many aspects of civilian society. However, the peculiar conditions of combat have obscured the extent to which morale leadership is especially required for military formations. This is not to imply that the military establishment has found a formula for appropriately balancing domination and manipulation.

c) NARROWING THE SKILL DIFFERENTIAL BETWEEN
    MILITARY AND CIVILIAN ELITES

The consequences of the new tasks of military management imply that the professional soldier is required more and more to acquire skills and orientations common to civilian administrators and even political leaders. He is more interested in the interpersonal techniques of organization, morale, negotiation, and symbolic interaction. He is forced to develop political orientations in order to explain the goals of military activities to his staff and subordinates. Not only must he have the skills necessary for internal management; he must develop a "public relations" aptitude, in order to relate his formation to other military formations and to civilian organizations. This is not to imply that these skills are found among all the top military professionals, but the concentration is indeed great and seems to be growing. The transferability of skills from the military establishment to civilian organizations is thereby increased. Within the military establishment, conflicts occur and deepen with greater acceleraion between the old, tradi-

tionally oriented officers and the new, who are more sensitized to
the emerging problems of morale and initiative.

Trends in Indoctrination

In the past, institutional indoctrination of the military professional in the United States avoided discussion of human factors
in the military establishment and the political consequences of
military operations. (It is, of course, difficult, if not impossible,
to intellectualize at any length about the enforcement of discipline.) Before World War II, the United States professional military had a schooling which supplied little realistic orientation
except to emphasize a simple mechanical version of ultimate civilian supremacy. However, even before the outbreak of World
War II, important sectors of the military elite had slowly and pain-
fully to reorient themselves on these matters. Reorientation came
about as a result of the realities of the war. Of course, much of
the crucial work merely devolved upon lower-rank staff officers
and technical specialists, with the "top military cadre" not fully
in sympathy.

In the absence of institutional indoctrination for these tasks,
impressive indeed is the extent to which self-indoctrination suc-
ceeded in producing officers capable of functioning in these areas.
Nevertheless, the military establishment continues to be characterized by deep inner tensions because of its new responsibilities and
because of the absence of a sufficiently large cadre of top officers
sensitized to deal effectively with its broad administrative and
political tasks.

Before World War II, whatever training and indoctrination
existed for handling the complexities of civil-military relations
and political tasks were primarily self-generated. Not only were
some deviant career officers sensitive to the emerging problems
within the military establishment, but many of these officers sought
to indoctrinate themselves about emerging problems of civil-
military relations and of the political aspects of military operations.
They often accepted specialized assignments of a quasi-politi-

cal nature or which involved communications skills that supplied relevant opportunities for indoctrination and training. (These
assignments included military attaché, foreign-language officer,
intelligence officer, and public relations.) Voluntary acceptance
or pursuit of these assignments represented genuine efforts at self-
indoctrination; thus, the choice selected out for training those who
felt inclined and had potential for growth. In the United States
especially, before 1939, these assignments had relatively low prestige. In fact, they were seen as interfering with one's career, and
therefore they were avoided by all except those who had sufficient
foresight to see their high relevance. For many, these assignments
did involve risk and short-term disadvantages. But the results of
such assignments in crucial cases were just the contrary. They
helped officers to enter the very top of the military elite, since
they did, in fact, represent realistic indoctrination for emerging
tasks.

Since the end of World War II, at all levels of the military establishment institutional indoctrination has encompassed much wider
perspectives, social and political. Although much of the new indoctrination appears to be oriented to the broader problems of the
military establishment — internal and external — it is very much
an open question what the consequences are likely to be for civil-
military relations in a democratic society.

Ideological indoctrination is now designed to eliminate the civilian contempt for the "military mind." The "military mind" has
been charged with traditionalism and a lack of inventiveness. The
new indoctrination stresses initiative and continuous innovation.
This is appropriate for the career motives of the new recruits and
is important in creating conditions for overcoming bureaucratic
inertia. The "military mind" has been charged with an inclination
toward ultra-nationalism and ethnocentrism. Professional soldiers
are being taught to de-emphasize ethnocentric thinking, since
ethnocentrism is detrimental to national and military policy. The
"military mind" has been charged with being disciplinarian. The
new indoctrination seeks to deal with human factors in combat

and in large-scale organization in a manner similar to current views on human relations in industry. In short, the new indoctrination is designed to supply the professional soldier with an opinion on all political, social, and economic subjects which his new role obliges him to hold.

The new "intellectualism" is a critical capacity and a critical orientation. The military officer must be realistic, and he must review the shortcomings of the past and current record of political-military relations. Will the growth of critical capacities be destructive, or will it be productive of new solutions? The consequence could be a growth in hostility toward past arrangements, in particular toward past political leadership of the military establishment and toward the dogma of civilian supremacy. The military profession runs the risk of confusing its technical competence with intellectual background. As a result, it could become critical and negative toward the military bureaucracy and toward civilian political leadership in the same way that Joseph Schumpeter speaks of the university-trained specialist's becoming critical of the economic system. In the United States, at least, such hostility is hardly likely to lead to open disaffection, but it may be conducive to passive resentment and bitterness.

In the long run, under either the democratic or the totalitarian model, the military establishment cannot be controlled and still remain effective by civilianizing it. Despite the growth of the logistical dimensions of warfare, the professional soldier is, in the last analysis, a military commander and not a business or organizational administrator. The democratic elite model of civilian supremacy must proceed on the assumption that the function of the professional military is to command soldiers into battle. There is no reason to believe that the characteristics of the ideal professional soldier as a military commander are compatible with the ideal professional soldier as an object of civilian control, although the differences seem to be growing less and less as the automation of war continues. The quality of political control of the professional soldier can be judged by examining not those aspects of the military establishment which are most civilian but rather those which are least civilian. Here the willingness to submit to civilian control, rather than the actuality of civilian control, is most crucial.

There is no reason to believe, in a democratic society, that the military can be controlled by offering it the conditions of employment found in civilian society. In the long run, civilian establishments would draw off all the best talent, especially in a business-dominated society. To achieve the objectives of the democratic elite model, it is necessary to maintain and build on the differentiation between civilian and military roles. A democratic society must accord the professional soldier a position based on his skill and on his special code of honor. He must be integrated because his fundamental differentiation is recognized. Under these circumstances, standards of behavior can be established and political directives enforced. The current drift toward destroying the differences between the military and the civilian cannot produce genuine similarity but runs the risk of creating new forms of hostility and unanticipated militarism.

ACKNOWLEDGMENTS

This essay is the outgrowth of my participation in the seminar work of the Committee for the Comparative Study of New Nations at the University of Chicago. The Committee, which seeks to bring a comparative approach to the study of new nations, was organized by Professors Edward A. Shils and David Apter under a grant from the Carnegie Corporation. Among its members are Professors Leonard Binder, Department of Political Science; Lloyd Fallers, Department of Anthropology; Clifford Geertz, Department of Anthropology, and Harry Johnson, Department of Economics. I wish to acknowledge their individual and collective assistance in preparing this study.

INDEX

Abrahamsson, Bengt, 22
Adelman, Irma, 24 n.
Afghanistan, 63, 64, 86, 89, 96, 98
Africa, 5, 10–11, 14, 34, 43, 44
Africa, Sub-Sahara, 35, 41, 52, 56–
    57, 58, 65–67, 85, 89, 90, 91,
    93; absence of feudalism, 126;
    colonial experience, 88, 90–91;
    cultural attitudes to military,
    120, 159; military expansionism,
    174, 175; military in politics,
    89, 141; military professional-
    ism, 132; military role in eco-
    nomic development, 152, 157–
    58
Africanization of officer corps, 82, 91,
    170
Air forces in new states, political
    potential, 109
Algeria, 33, 60, 86, 96; military re-
    cruitment, 129
al-Salal, Brigadier Abdullah, 163
Andrews, William G., 52 n.
Angola, 174
Arab-Israeli conflict, 19. *See also*
    Yom Kippur war
Arab League, 174
Argentina, 67–68, 69
Asceticism among military, 139, 140,
    143
Asia, 5, 10–11, 14, 35, 41, 43, 44,
    52, 57, 61, 63, 64–65. *See also*

South and Southeast Asia
Ataturk. *See* Kemal Ataturk
Authoritarian–mass party system, 81,
    98, 99, 162, 179; defined, 82;
    elites, 188; separation of mili-
    tary and police, 115
Authoritarian–one party system, 81,
    98, 99, 162, 179; defined, 82;
    elites in, 188; military-police
    function, 115
Ayoub Khan, Mohammed, 64

Bangladesh, 43, 46, 63, 64
Banks, Arthur S., 27 n.
Be'eri, Eliezer, 52 n.
Belgium, colonial policies of, 90
Ben Bella, Ahmed, 60
Bienen, Henry, 4 n., 64 n., 66 n.
Bolivia, 51
Boumédienne, Houari, 60
Brazil, 34, 43, 57, 67, 68
Brinton, Crane, 8–9
Burma, 43, 63, 64, 83, 86, 96, 163,
    165, 171; military and economic
    development, 152–53, 154; mili-
    tary recruitment, 129, 131 n.;
    military and social ·cohesion,
    144, 145; military takeover,
    168–69
Burunda, 87, 97
Bury, Douglas P., 24 n.